Absolutely Epic

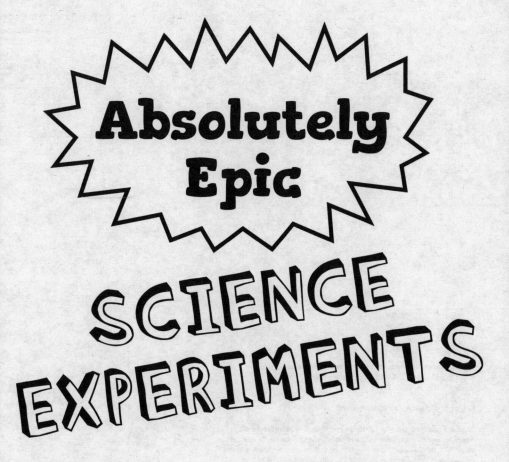

SCIENCE EXPERIMENTS

This edition published in 2022 by Arcturus Publishing Limited
26/27 Bickels Yard, 151–153 Bermondsey Street,
London SE1 3HA

Authors: Anna Claybourne and Anne Rooney
Cover artwork: Luke Seguin-Magee
Illustrations: Caroline Romanet and Shutterstock
Editor: Donna Gregory
Designer: Marie Everitt

CH008633NT
Supplier 10, Date 0122, Print run 11499

Printed in the UK

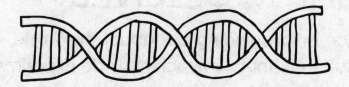

CONTENTS

WHAT IS SCIENCE?

Science means finding out about the world, and all the stuff in it. That's why scientists do experiments—to find out as much as they can! The science you learn in this book will help you understand our world.

The chapter on **forces** is about how things move. These jet planes fly by pushing gas out behind them, like the balloon rocket in this book.

Scientists studying **materials** look at the "stuff" around us. Have you ever wondered why ice floats? It's because when water freezes, it takes up more space—so ice is lighter than water.

Energy makes things happen. These solar panels collect light energy from the Sun and turn it into another form of energy—electricity!

Plants and animals are both **living things**. Wheat needs plenty of sunlight and rain to grow well. What about you? What do you need to stay healthy?

BEFORE STARTING

- Clear a tidy, empty space for doing experiments in.
- Check that it's OK to use the things in the "You will need" boxes with whoever owns them!
- For messy experiments, wear old clothes, not your best outfit!
- Do messy experiments outdoors, if you can.
- Remember to clean up the mess after!

GET AN ADULT ASSISTANT

For some of the experiments, you'll need to heat things, cook things, chop things up, or use electrical items. For anything like this, make sure you have an adult handy to help you.

TRY IT YOURSELF!

This book is full of easy but exciting experiments for you to try for yourself. For most of them, you only need a few basic things that you can find at home.

KEEPING RECORDS

Real scientists don't just do experiments—they also keep records. To do this, you could take photos of your experiments. or draw pictures of your experiments, and write down what happened.

Are you ready? Then let's get started ... with experiments about FORCES!

CHAPTER 1

Experiments with Forces

FORCES

How do you make a tower of bricks fall over?
Push it! How do you get a toboggan up a hill?
Pull it! These pushes and pulls are called forces.
They are everywhere, making things around us
move, stop, or change shape.

PUSH

A push can make something move, like when you push a scooter along with your foot. Pushes can also make things fall over or get squashed—like when you squeeze clay.

PULL

A pull can make something move, like when you pull a plug out of the sink. It can also make something stretch, like a rubber band.

Working together

There is often more than one force at work at the same time. The push of the bat makes a ball fly forward. At the same time, gravity pulls it down.

Try this!

Take two toy cars, and zoom them toward each other at high speed. Your hand pushes a car and makes it move. The cars stop when they push against each other. The cars may fly up in the air, but then gravity pulls them back down.

GRAVITY

Gravity is a pulling force between objects. The Earth is a huge object that has lots of gravity. So when you jump up, the Earth's gravity pulls you down again.

FRICTION

Friction is a dragging force. It makes things slow down or grip when they rub on each other. Bike brakes use friction to slow down the wheels. Tennis shoe soles use friction to grip the ground.

SPOON SHOOTER

Have you ever tried to throw an apple to a friend, or taken a shot at a basketball hoop? You have to get it just right!

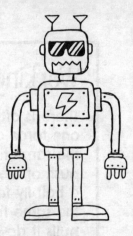

You will need:

- A long wooden or metal spoon
- A ruler
- Rubber bands
- Balled-up pairs of socks
- Scrunched-up paper balls
- A plastic bowl

1

1 Lay the spoon on top of the ruler, with the ends of the ruler and the spoon handle lining up. Loop several rubber bands tightly around the handle end to hold them firmly together.

2 Stuff one or two pairs of socks between the spoon and the ruler, close to the rubber bands. This will make the curved end of the spoon stick up.

3 Put the plastic bowl a short distance away. This will be your target to shoot at. Make some scrunched-up paper cannonballs.

4 Put a cannonball in the spoon. Holding the ruler still, gently push down the bowl end of the spoon.

5 To shoot the cannonball, let the spoon go, so that it flips back up. Fire!

Another fun idea

What else will your spoon shooter shoot? Try table tennis balls, marshmallows, or raisins (but you might want to avoid anything too hard or messy!).

WHAT HAS HAPPENED?

As the spoon flips back up, it pushes your cannonball into the air. Friction with the air slows the ball down. As it slows, gravity pulls it to the ground. This creates a smooth, curved path through the air. When you aim, you have to balance your pushing force with the way friction and gravity will work, to get that curve exactly right. When you do——PLOP! A hole in one!

DID YOU KNOW?

Some people are "human calculators" and can do really complicated sums in their heads instantly—even faster than someone with a calculator! No one knows exactly how their brains are different.

Malaria is a tropical disease spread by mosquitoes. Since the Stone Age, malaria has been responsible for half of all human deaths from illness.

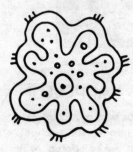

Each person's tongue print is unique.

In ancient times, Indian doctors used live ants to "stitch" wounds together. The doctor would hold the edges together and get the ant to bite through the skin. The ant's head would then be snapped off, leaving its jaws as the "stitch!"

If scientists could build a brain from computer chips, it would take a million times as much power to run as a real human brain.

Your brain receives about 100 million pieces of information at any one moment from your eyes, nose, ears, skin, and receptors inside your body.

Eating asparagus produces a chemical that makes urine smell strongly, although not everyone can smell it. Lucky them!

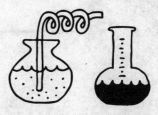

A sneeze travels at 161 km (100 miles) per hour.

A body left unburied in a tropical climate will be reduced to a skeleton in two weeks by the action of insects.

People can be born with ears growing from their necks.

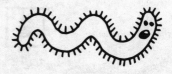

There are more bacteria in your mouth than there are people in the whole world!

15

BALLOON ROCKET

What makes a rocket blast off into space? Rockets push gases out of their engines. The gas pushes back, and this makes the rocket move. Make this model balloon rocket to see how it works.

You will need:

- A balloon
- A straw
- A long piece of thin string
- Tape
- Several assistants!

1 Cut a piece of string 3-4 m (10-13 ft) long. Thread the straw onto it.

2 Ask two people to hold the ends of the string and pull it tight. (Or you could tie it to something.)

3

Blow up the balloon. Don't knot the end—just firmly hold it closed.

4

While you hold it, ask someone to tape the balloon to the straw, like this.

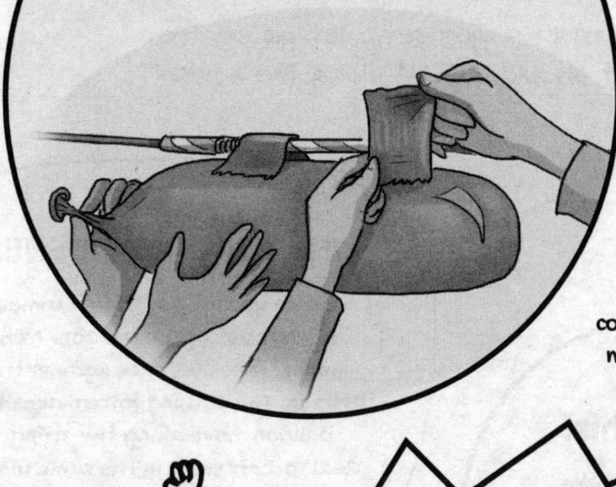

continues on next page

Another fun idea

Can you make two teams, each with their own balloon rocket, and have a race?

5 Move the balloon and straw along to the end of the string, with the open end of the balloon pointing back.

6 On your marks, get set ... let go of the balloon! It should ZOOM along the string!

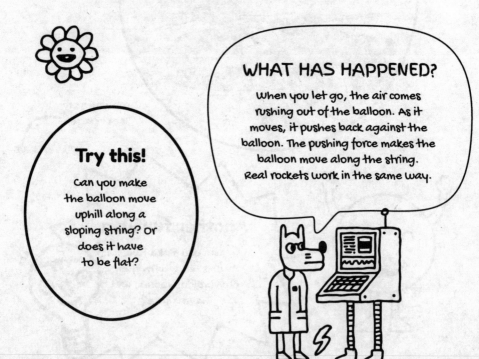

WHAT HAS HAPPENED?

When you let go, the air comes rushing out of the balloon. As it moves, it pushes back against the balloon. The pushing force makes the balloon move along the string. Real rockets work in the same way.

Try this!

Can you make the balloon move uphill along a sloping string? Or does it have to be flat?

DID YOU KNOW?

Robotarium X in Portugal is the first zoo full of robots, where 45 robots share a steel and glass cage. Some are nice, and respond to visitors. Others are nasty and bite the tails off their companions. How bizarre!

The dandyhorse was an early form of bicycle in the 1930s. It had no pedals, and you had to push it along by foot.

"Frozen smoke" is a solid that is 99 percent air—its real name is aerogel. It looks transparent but hazy—just like frozen smoke!

By adding vinegar to red cabbage when you cook it, you can make it go pink. Add some bicarbonate of soda to make it turn blue instead.

When a gas pipeline leaks in the California desert, workers put a chemical into the gas that attracts vultures. The vultures gather where the gas leaks out, so workers only need to spot the vultures to find the leak.

The world's largest working smart phone is called the Maxi Handy and is 2.05 m (6.72 ft) tall!

19

MARBLE RUN

A marble can roll all the way through a maze by itself—as long as the force of gravity is pulling it. Make your own marble run, and watch the marbles roll down to the end!

You will need:

- Marbles
- Several card-board tubes from rolls of paper towel or toilet paper
- Scissors
- A cupboard door that you can put tape on
- Tape
- Basket or box

1 Carefully cut along the sides of the tubes to make each one into two curved marble tracks.

2 Start making a path for your marbles by taping the tracks to a cupboard door or refrigerator.

Another fun idea

Can you make a 3D, free-standing marble run? Use whole cardboard tubes as towers. See if you can link them all together.

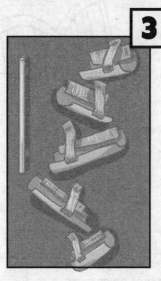

3

Tape along the side of each track, then add a bit more tape over the top to make it stronger.

4

Each track must slope down and lead to another track. Use as many as you can to make a path for the marbles from top to bottom. Put a basket at the bottom to collect the marbles. Now, hold a marble at the starting point and then let it roll!

Can you time how long your marble takes? Does it speed up as it goes?

5

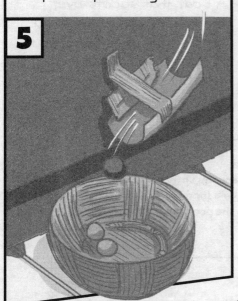

WHAT HAS HAPPENED?

The Earth's gravity pulls down on things all the time. If there is a flat surface in the way, it stops them from falling. But if the surface is sloped, objects can get pulled down the slope, toward Earth. Balls, such as marbles, move downhill very easily, because they roll instead of sliding.

DID YOU KNOW?

There is no benefit in using striped toothpaste—the stripes are purely to make the toothpaste look more interesting.

It's impossible to fold a dry piece of paper in half more than seven times.

A boat that scoots over the waves, and looks like a giant spider, was launched in 2007. It can travel 8,000 km (5,000 miles) on one tank of diesel fuel.

If you were to stroke a cat 70 million times, you would generate enough static electricity to power a 60-watt light bulb for one minute. Don't try this one at home ... the poor cat would have no hair left!

Dropping, heating, or hammering a magnet can reduce its magnetic power.

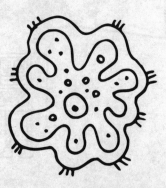

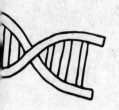

The National Institute for Standards and Technology in the USA has made an atomic clock as small as a grain of rice.

Aconite is one of the most deadly poisons known—yet it is used in homeopathic remedies as a medicine!

In 2001 surgeons in New York used a robot to successfully remove the gall bladder from a patient in France.

Using sonar equipment, scientists can detect the sounds made by fin whales and blue whales from 850 km (350 miles) away.

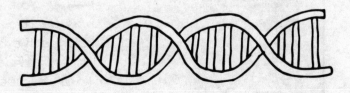

BALANCING SHAPES

If you spread your arms out, you can balance on one tiptoe—for a little while! Balancing depends on how gravity pulls on objects. Try balancing these shapes. You might be amazed!

You will need:

- Tracing paper
- Pens
- Card
- Scissors
- Small coins
- Tape
- Thin string

BALANCING BUTTERFLY

1 Trace this butterfly, cut it out, and draw around it onto a piece of card.

2 Cut out your butterfly and use pens to decorate it. Tape two small coins under the front wing tips in the circles shown.

3 You should now be able to balance the butterfly on your finger by the tip of its nose.

TIGHTROPE CLOWN

1 Trace the clown, cut it out, and draw around it onto a piece of card.

2 Decorate your clown and then cut it out. Tape two coins under her hands.

3 Make a tightrope by tying some string across a gap, or ask someone to hold the string up. See if your clown will balance upside down on her bow tie!

WHAT HAS HAPPENED?

Objects balance because their weight is spread out evenly around a central point. If the object rests line with this point, it balances. You would expect these clown shapes to fall, but the coins move the shapes' balance point, making them balance.

DID YOU KNOW?

If a glass of water were magnified to the size of the whole Earth, each molecule would be the size of a tennis ball. Juan Jimenez in Puerto Rico, USA, owns the smallest jet aircraft. It measures 3.7 m (12 ft) in length, weighs 162 kg (358 lbs) and can travel at speeds of 483 km (300 miles) per hour!

Reports of ghosts have dropped considerably as the use of smartphones has increased. It seems that the spooks don't like the radio waves!

The water you drink has been through many other people's bodies before it gets to you. But don't worry—it's been cleaned!

An early model of a hovercraft was made from an empty cat food tin, a vacuum cleaner, and a coffee tin!

Scientists are testing the use of blue lights to help keep night drivers awake. They work by convincing the human body clock that it's morning!

Golf balls can sometimes reach speeds of 273 km (170 miles) per hour.

A FogScreen is a curtain of fog onto which you can project images from a computer or video. Using a FogScreen, it's possible to show a movie anywhere.

If you whirl a bucket of water around fast enough, the water will not fall out even when the bucket is upside down! This is caused because the centrifugal force (that pushes objects outward) is greater than the force of gravity, which would normally cause the water to fall.

Percy Spencer (USA) invented the microwave oven in 1945, using new technology developed for military purposes during World War II.

A traditional old recipe for plant fertilizer consisted of rotten cow dung, ground up bones and dry blood. In fact, you can still get any or all of these from a garden store to make your own. Or you could just buy a bottle of fertilizer ...

MAGIC MAGAZINES!

How hard can a magazine hold on? You're about to find out!

You will need:

- Two old magazines or large, thick paperback books. The more pages, the better!

1 Lay the magazines down next to each other and open them out.

2 Put the front page of one magazine over the back page of the other. Then fold down a page from the first magazine, then a page from the other, and so on.

3

Keep folding down the pages of the magazines until they are all used up. Press the magazines tightly closed.

4 Try to pull the magazines apart. Why is it so hard?!?

WHAT HAS HAPPENED?

The rough paper pages have a lot of friction—a dragging, gripping force. When they rub against each other, they grip and hold tight. You could easily pull two or four pages apart. But when all the pages are together, there's so much friction that they hold on very tightly.

DID YOU KNOW?

If an electric current is applied to two glasses of water standing next to each other, with the positive electrode in one glass and the negative in the other, the water will climb up the walls of the glass and form a bridge between the two glasses in mid-air to allow the current to flow.

Radar was first used to detect enemy aircraft during World War II.

The gas used for cookers and fires has no smell. The gas supply company adds the strong smell deliberately so that people can tell immediately if there is a leak.

Doctors in ancient Egypt would give patients an electric shock with a catfish to treat the pain caused by arthritis.

Commonwealth Bay in Antarctica has the strongest winds of anywhere in the world—they blow at up to 322 km (200 miles) per hour.

Many types of toothpaste contain the skeletons of microscopic creatures from the sea, called diatoms.

An android (human-like robot) has recently been designed with light sensors behind its eyes, so it can follow a person's movements. There are others who can "breathe," move, and talk like humans.

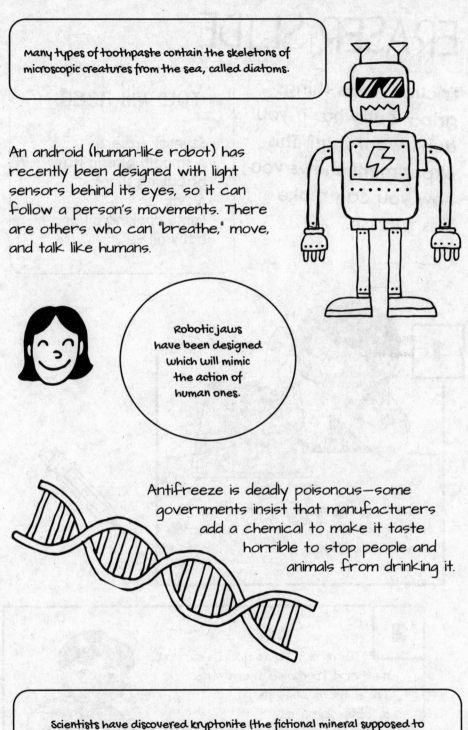

Robotic jaws have been designed which will mimic the action of human ones.

Antifreeze is deadly poisonous—some governments insist that manufacturers add a chemical to make it taste horrible to stop people and animals from drinking it.

Scientists have discovered kryptonite (the fictional mineral supposed to deprive Superman of his powers) in a mine in Siberia. The mineral, called sodium lithium boron silicate hydroxide, exactly matches the formula of kryptonite in the film Superman Returns.

ERASER SLIDE

Friction helps things grip—but what if you don't want that? This experiment shows you how you can make less friction.

You will need:

- Several erasers
- A smooth plastic tray or baking sheet
- A box
- Some cooking oil or baby oil

1

Make a gentle slope by propping the tray up on the box. Try sliding some erasers down it.

2

Erasers have good friction; it's hard to make them slide. Take them off, then dribble some oil over your tray slide.

3 Now try again. Do the erasers slide more easily?

Another fun idea

Try holding a plastic bottle full of water with dry hands, wet hands, and oily hands.

WHAT HAS HAPPENED?

The erasers and the tray grip each other as they rub together. When you add a layer of liquid oil, it flows in between them and separates them. That makes it much harder for them to grip.

DID YOU KNOW?

The world's smallest cinema was built in 1934 and used to use bed sheets as a screen! The *Cinema Dei Piccoli* in Rome, Italy was restored in 1991 and has 63 seats, air conditioning, and stereo sound. The bed sheets have been upgraded, too!

People in Pakistan have been visiting the dentist for 9,000 years. Archeologists have found drilled and capped teeth in ancient skeletons discovered there.

Glow sticks are the only safe form of lighting to use straight after an earthquake. They produce light from the reaction of chemicals sealed inside the stick.

Irons have been used for centuries and used to be heated up in the oven! The first electric ones appeared in 1891.

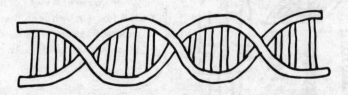

Wearing an asbestos suit lined with reflective foil, a fire fighter can survive temperatures of 1,093 °C (2,000 °F).

Salt is the only rock that humans can eat.

It's possible to locate a person using a smartphone with almost pinpoint accuracy, wherever they are in the world.

Human bodies decay more slowly than they used to, as food is now packed with preservatives that make their way into the flesh—and preserve us, too!

The gas inside most light bulbs is not air, but another gas called argon.

DOES WATER HAVE SKIN?

Pins and needles are made of metal. Drop them in water, and they'll sink. But if you are very careful, you can make them sit on the water's surface. It's as if a "skin" holds them up!

You will need:

- Coins, pins and needles, and paper clips or small safety pins
- A large bowl of water
- Paper towel

ON THE WATER

1 Let the water in your bowl settle until it is still. Drop in a pin or needle, pointing downward. What happens?

2 Now place a pin or needle flat on the surface. If it's tricky, try resting it on some paper towel. Does your pin float on the water?

THE BULGING COIN

1 Put a coin down on the tabletop.

2 Dip your finger in your bowl of water. Start dripping drops of water onto the coin.

3 Carefully drip more and more drops onto the coin. What happens? How many drops can you add?

WHAT HAS HAPPENED?

Water does not actually have a skin. But water molecules—the tiny parts that make up water—have a pulling force. They pull together extra hard on the water surface. This is called surface tension. It gives water a "skin" that objects can rest on, as you can see in the first experiment. It also pulls water together, as you can see in the second test, when the water piles up in a big bulge.

DID YOU KNOW?

A robotic caterpillar controlled by a joystick can be inserted through a small hole in the chest, and crawl over a person's heart to inject drugs or install implants to heal any damage.

Russian scientists are experimenting with concrete submarines. They would not show up on sonar displays, as they would look the same as rocks or sand.

Bubbles of gas produced by bacteria form the holes in Swiss cheese.

In terms of its size, a laser is a brighter light than the Sun.

An average household's annual waste contains enough unreleased energy to power a television for 5,000 hours.

Pykrete is a rock-hard solid made of frozen water and sawdust. It is ten times tougher than just ordinary ice and melts more slowly.

If you bend a piece of dry spaghetti until it breaks, it will always fall into more than two pieces.

Roman engineers were ahead of their time. They heated chalk and seashells at over 900 °C (1,650 °F) to make lime, to which they added volcanic ash, to make concrete.

Diamonds are made from the same chemical as the lead in pencils, but the atoms are arranged differently.

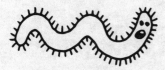

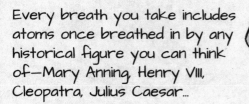

Every breath you take includes atoms once breathed in by any historical figure you can think of—Mary Anning, Henry VIII, Cleopatra, Julius Caesar...

DIVING BELL

Before submarines and scuba gear, people used a diving bell to breathe underwater. How did it work?

1

Tear a small strip off the paper handkerchief. Wrap it around the toy figure like a bandage, and use the rubber band or thread to hold it on.

2

Put the toy inside the glass. Use a blob of play clay to stick its head to the base of the glass.

3

Turn the glass upside down, and push it into the water until it touches the bottom.

4 Can you see what's happening inside the glass? Is it filling up with water?

5

Keeping the glass upside down, carefully lift it out. Dry your hands, and remove the toy. If it has stayed dry, the paper handkerchief will not be damp.

WHAT HAS HAPPENED?

You can't see air, but it takes up space and has a pushing force, called air pressure. The air trapped inside the glass pushes down, so that water cannot get in. The toy stays dry inside. If it were alive, it would be able to breathe the air for a while, too. People used to go underwater in much bigger diving bells.

DID YOU KNOW?

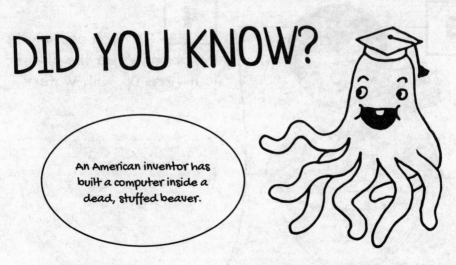

An American inventor has built a computer inside a dead, stuffed beaver.

The world's tallest limousine was built in Australia and measures 3.33 m (10 ft 11 in.) from floor to roof. It took 4,000 hours to build it.

Two American scientists have made a computer mouse that is fitted inside the skin of a real, dead mouse. Gross!

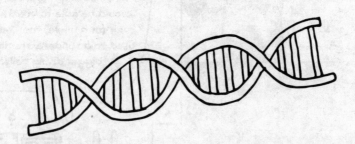

An Australian scientist started a long experiment in 1927 to prove that pitch (a sticky black substance used for waterproofing boats and roofs) is not solid, but a very thick liquid. He put some pitch in a funnel and left it to drip through—by 1995, only seven drops had fallen through the funnel!

A company in the USA has developed a luminescent computer keyboard which allows you to type in the dark!

Edwin A. Shackleton (UK) has flown in 843 different types of aircraft. He reached this total in January 2007 and holds the world record.

Pigeons won't land on a statue that contains the metal gallium. A Japanese scientist is developing a spray containing gallium that can be used to treat buildings to keep them free from bird droppings.

The slime produced by a slug produces a small electric current when smeared over copper. Slug-powered smartphone, anyone?

FUN WITH MAGNETS

Magnets have a special kind of force, called magnetism. They can pull some metal objects toward them, as if by magic.

You will need:

- One or more strong magnets
- Metal paper clips
- String
- Tape
- Thin card
- Pen

ANTIGRAVITY PAPER CLIPS

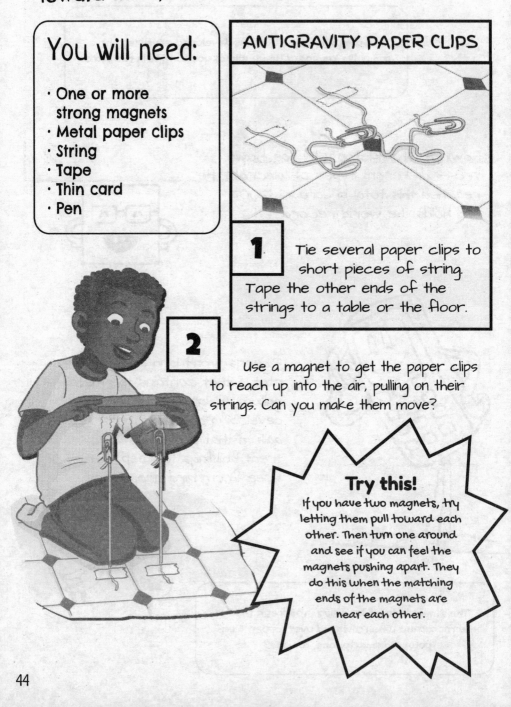

1 Tie several paper clips to short pieces of string. Tape the other ends of the strings to a table or the floor.

2 Use a magnet to get the paper clips to reach up into the air, pulling on their strings. Can you make them move?

Try this!

If you have two magnets, try letting them pull toward each other. Then turn one around and see if you can feel the magnets pushing apart. They do this when the matching ends of the magnets are near each other.

STRING OF CLIPS

1 Hold a magnet up and put a paper clip close to it, so that it clings to the magnet.

2 Hold another paper clip near that paper clip to see if it will cling on. Add another and another. How long can you make your string of clips?

MAGIC MAZE

1 Draw a maze on a piece of card. Put a paper clip on top of the card and the magnet underneath.

2 Can you use the magnet to make the clip move through the maze?

WHAT HAS HAPPENED?

Magnets can pull on some types of metal and on other magnets. When a metal object, such as a paper clip, is touching a magnet, it becomes a magnet, too. Magnetism is invisible, and it can work across empty space and through other things, such as card or plastic.

DID YOU KNOW?

The walking or stilt palm walks to a better spot if it doesn't like where it's living! The tree grows up to 21 m (70 ft) tall in the Amazon. Stilts hold it up and support its central trunk. To move, the tree grows more stilts on one side, and then lets the other ones die so that it slowly moves along.

The first railroads were built in Germany around 1550.

Plastic can take up to 500 years to decompose.

One of the latest advances in technology is a slugbot—a robot designed to hunt down slugs!

At temperatures below about minus 25 °C (minus 13 °F), bubbles can freeze in the air and shatter when hitting the ground.

About 20 percent of the world's electricity comes from hydroelectric power (power generated from flowing water).

The heat of chilli peppers is measured in Scoville heat units. The world's hottest chilli pepper is the *Bhut Jolokia* from India, at 577,000 units.

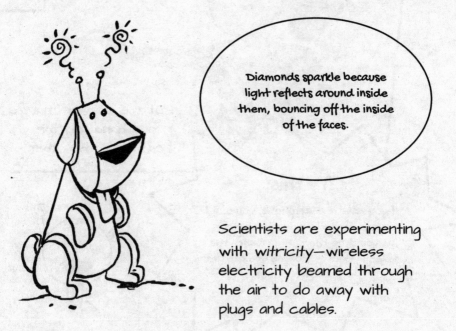

Diamonds sparkle because light reflects around inside them, bouncing off the inside of the faces.

Scientists are experimenting with witricity—wireless electricity beamed through the air to do away with plugs and cables.

THE SPEED OF GRAVITY

How fast does gravity pull things down? Does it depend on how heavy they are?

You will need:

- A feather
- A coin or marble
- Two matching plastic or cardboard tube containers with lids
- Food scale

1 Check that the coin or marble feels heavier than the feather—it should be. If you have a set of kitchen scales, you could weigh them both.

2 Put the coin or marble in one hand and the feather in the other.

Try this!

If you have a smartphone, you could ask someone to video the objects as you drop them. Then watch the video in slow motion, so you can get a really good look.

3 Drop the coin or marble and the feather, making sure you let go of them at exactly the same time. Which hits the ground first?

4

Now put the coin or marble inside one container and the feather inside the other. Close the lids. Check that the container with the marble inside is still heavier than the one with the feather inside.

WHAT HAS HAPPENED?

When the objects are not inside the containers, the feather falls more slowly—but when they are, they fall at the same speed. Gravity pulls lighter and heavier objects at the same speed. However, in air, a light, fluffy object—say, a feather—will get slowed down more by the air in its way. This is called air resistance, a type of force.

5 Hold out both containers, and drop them at exactly the same time as before. Now which one hits the ground first?

DID YOU KNOW?

Hawaii has a beach with green sand. It's the only one known, and was produced by olivine—a volcanic rock that smashed into tiny grains.

In the last 550 million years, there have been five events that have each destroyed at least 50 percent of all life on the planet.

Some rocks float on water. Pumice stone is hardened volcanic lava. It often contains so many air bubbles that it is light enough to float.

Fossilized sea animals are often found on the tops of tall mountains. The mountain tops were once parts of the seabed that have been pushed upward by colliding lumps of land.

For 186 days of the year, the Sun is not visible at the North Pole.

When lightning strikes a beach, it melts the sand, which hardens again as a type of glass called fulgurite. It often forms in twisty tube shapes.

The world's tallest mountain looks quite flat! Mauna Kea in Hawaii is 10,205 m (33,480 ft) tall from its base on the seabed, but 60 percent of it is hidden under the sea and the rest doesn't look very pointy!

Earth is gradually getting thicker around the middle, becoming more pumpkin-shaped than round.

Nearly an eighth of the Earth's surface is dry desert where less than 25 cm (10 in) of rain falls in a year.

The largest desert in the world also contains most of the world's fresh water! Antarctica qualifies as a desert as it has virtually no rainfall.

BOTTLE BALL

It should be easy to blow a paper ball into a bottle, right? Wrong!

You will need:

- A large empty plastic water bottle
- A scrunched-up paper ball, smaller than the bottle neck

1

Set the bottle down flat on a table. Gently put the paper ball just inside the bottle neck.

Try this!

Can you make the ball go into the bottle by sucking air out of the bottle with a straw?

2 Challenge a friend to blow the ball into the bottle— or try doing it yourself! It's impossible.

IMPOSSIBLE!

WHAT HAS HAPPENED?

The bottle has no liquid in it, but it's not empty—it's full of air. When you blow into it, you add even more air. The air pushes its way back out of the bottle and pushes the ball out, too.

Now try this!

Does it make any difference if you use bottles of different sizes? What about bottles made of different materials, such as plastic or glass?

DID YOU KNOW?

The aurora borealis, or Northern lights are displays of swirling green, red, and other hues high in the night sky near the North Pole. They're caused by charged particles from the solar wind hitting atoms from the Earth's atmosphere, making them emit light in swirling patterns.

Brazil is home to 30 percent of the rain forest left on Earth.

Tough little tadpoles of some species of frog are able to live inside a pitcher plant without being dissolved by its acidic juices.

A Venus flytrap is a carnivorous plant that traps and eats flies. It doesn't strike quickly—it takes half an hour to squash a fly and kill it, and another ten days to digest it.

In 1976, children playing in their school playground found their heads began to glow. It was an appearance of St Elmo's fire—a glow caused by the build-up of static electricity before a thunderstorm.

Some types of bamboo grow up to 91 cm (35 in) a day. This means they are growing at a rate of 0.00003 km (0.00002 miles) per hour!

The most poisonous plant in the world is the castor bean. Just 70 micrograms (2 millionths of an ounce) is enough to kill an adult human. It's 12,000 times more poisonous than rattlesnake venom.

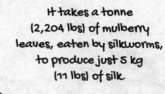

It takes a tonne (2,204 lbs) of mulberry leaves, eaten by silkworms, to produce just 5 kg (11 lbs) of silk.

Potatoes are the roots of the potato plant. They are where all the plant's energy is stored.

The bark of the redwood tree can't burn. When there are wildfires in redwood forests, it is the inside of the tree that burns!

A prickly cycad (a type of plant) brought to Kew Gardens in London in 1775 is still alive, more than 230 years later.

CHAPTER 2

Experiments
with Materials

MATERIALS

Reach out your hand and touch something. Wherever you are, whatever you're doing, you'll be surrounded by real, 3D stuff that you can feel. There are many different types of this stuff, known as "materials."

USEFUL MATERIALS

We need materials for making things. Without them, we wouldn't have homes, clothes, computers, or anything else. But when we use materials, we have to pick the right one for the job. The properties of each material decide what it can be used for.

Socks are made out of strong, soft threads, like cotton or wool. What would be a really bad thing to make socks out of?

Try this!

Find a pen and paper. Set a timer for 2 minutes. In that time, how many different materials can you find in your home or classroom (or wherever you happen to be)? Write them down.

TYPES OF MATERIALS

All the things around us are made of materials. There are thousands of types of materials. Here are just a few of them. Some materials are found in nature and are easy to find.

Water

Shells

Rocks

Wood

Some materials come from nature, but we have to get them out, or extract them.

Iron
(comes from some types of rocks)

Sunflower oil
(from sunflower seeds)

Cotton
(from the cotton plant)

Some materials are made by humans, using the natural materials we find around us.

Paper

Plastic

Paint

Concrete

PROPERTIES

Each material has its own properties —how it behaves and what it can do. For example, bamboo is strong and light. Rubber is bendy and tough.

TESTING, TESTING!

To find out what a material's properties are, scientists have to do tests. How strong is it? How stretchy is it? Is it waterproof? Is it see-through? Try testing some materials yourself!

You will need:

- A selection of small everyday objects. Here are some ideas, but you could use other things too:
    Coin
    Wooden matchstick
    Seashell
    Cork
    Metal paper clip
    Plastic button
    Eraser
    Small piece of paper
    Plastic sandwich bag
    Small carrot
    Sponge
    Rubber band
    Square of chocolate
    Sock
- A dishwashing bowl or bucket full of water
- A magnet

TEST 1: BEND OR BREAK?

Can you tear, break, or rip the object with your hands?

Try putting each object into the bowl or bucket of water, to see if it floats or not.

Tip!

These objects will endure some tough testing. So try not to use anything precious that you're not allowed to break!

In the charts

Real scientists write down what happens in their experiments. You could make a chart for each test to show your results.

Object	Floats	Does not float!
Coin		√
Matchstick	√	
Seashell		√
Cork	√	

61

TEST 3: THE MAGNET TEST

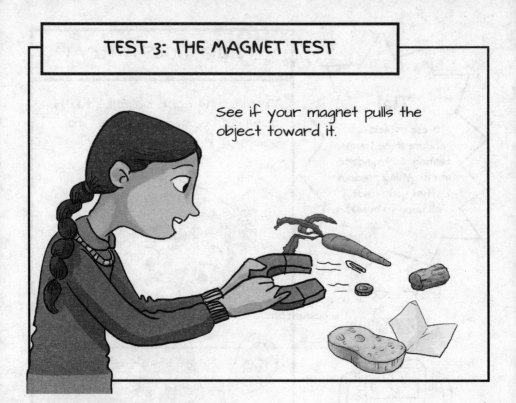

See if your magnet pulls the object toward it.

WHAT HAS HAPPENED?

Each material has its own properties, depending on what it is made of and how it is made. For example, a thin piece of wood is easy to snap, but a coin isn't. Cork floats easily, but a seashell will sink. What would each material be good for making?

Try this!

Can you think of any other tests you could try?

DID YOU KNOW?

Astronauts wear absorbant underwear during take off, landing, and on space walks, as they can't go to the bathroom at these times!

A giant squid washed up in Canada in 1878 had a body that was 6 m (20 ft) long with tentacles that measured up to 10.7 m (35 ft) long.

Potatoes are from the same family of plants as deadly nightshade. If the potato were to be discovered now, it would probably not be approved as a food!

Some types of rubber can be stretched to 1,000 times their original length.

An albatross can glide without flapping its wings for six days, given the right wind conditions.

Nicholas Joseph Cugnot designed the first car in France in 1769. It ran on steam and on rails!

In a magnetic material (such as iron) tiny groups of atoms line up, each with a North and South pole of their own, like miniature magnets.

MELTED CRAYON ART

Materials can change as they heat up and cool down. This is called "changing state." Try this experiment to see how crayons melt and harden again—and make some art, too!

You will need:

- Old wax crayons
- A hair dryer (and an adult to help)
- Strong tape
- A thick, stiff piece of card (white is best)
- Newspaper

1 Tape several crayons along the top of the card, pointing downward. Lean the card up against a wall or chair, with newspaper underneath to catch any drips.

Try this!

If you don't have a hair dryer, try leaving the card in hot sunshine or near a radiator. Make sure you check it's safe with an adult.

2

Switch on the hair dryer, and blow hot air at the crayons for a minute or two.

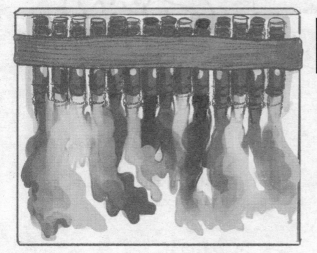

3

As the crayons start to melt and drip, tip the card to help the runny wax make patterns. Let the picture cool.

WHAT HAS HAPPENED?

As the crayons melt, they change from a solid into a liquid and run down the page. When they cool, the wax turns solid again.

DID YOU KNOW?

Geysers are fountains of hot water, sometimes above boiling point. The water is heated by molten rock under the Earth's crust, and then bubbles up to the surface under great pressure.

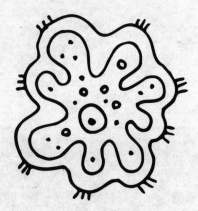

The Antarctic ice sheet contains 90 percent of all the fresh water on Earth.

Sound travels through granite rock ten times faster than it travels through air.

Oil and coal are both made from the dead bodies of animals and plants that lived millions of years ago.

The effects of global warming can be extreme—rising temperatures may lead to catastrophic floods, and droughts could destroy many plants, animals, and humans in years to come.

The Earth's crust—the solid surface of the Earth that holds the land and sea—is extremely thin. If the Earth were an apple, the crust would be about the thickness of the skin.

Obsidian is a naturally occurring shiny black glass, made when volcanic lava cools very fast. Its edges are razor sharp.

There is a super volcano underneath Yellowstone Park, USA, that last erupted 640,000 years ago. If it erupted now, ash would be thrown over the whole of the USA and the entire world's climate would change—perhaps enough to wipe out humans completely.

Enough energy reaches the Earth from the Sun every second to fulfil all our power needs for a year.

The Grand Canyon, USA, was created up to 14,000 years ago by the force of water rushing over the rock as the ice melted at the end of the last ice age.

THE SHRINKING PUDDLE

Materials can also change from a liquid into a gas. Gases are very spread out and can disappear into the air. Watch this happen with a puddle!

You will need:

- Some water
- A bowl
- An outdoor space
- A dry, warm, sunny day
- Chalk

1 Fill up a bowl with some water. Pour a little on the ground to make a puddle.

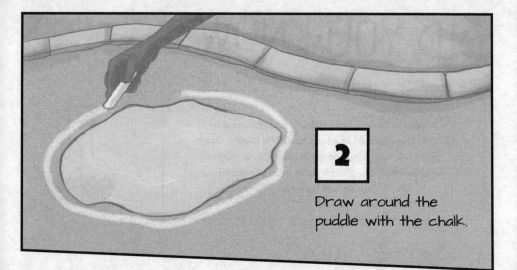

2

Draw around the puddle with the chalk.

3

Keep checking the puddle every half and hour or so. Draw around it each time.

WHAT HAS HAPPENED?

As the Sun and ground heat the water, it slowly turns into a gas, or "evaporates." The gas escapes into the air. The puddle shrinks from the edges, because more heat can reach there from the surrounding ground.

DID YOU KNOW?

A lake in Chile mysteriously disappeared in 2007. The glacial lake had water under a crust of ice. But at some point in 2007, the water disappeared completely and only chunks of ice were left behind.

If you lie in the Dead Sea, you float very easily! The sea is nine times as salty as the Mediterranean—too salty for fish to live in—but great to float in!

Lake Vostok lies buried under 4 km (2.5 miles) of ice in Antarctica, yet is full of liquid water. It was last open to the air around half a million years ago and was discovered by radar in 1994.

The Sahara desert has an aridity score of 200—that means it loses 200 times the amount of water that it gains!

Scientists in Colorado, USA, spent decades trying to help restock rivers with an endangered fish, but they used the wrong one! Many of the fish they released into the rivers were just ordinary fish that looked like the endangered one!

You can die of thirst in the desert in only two days. You'd need to drink 9 L (about 16 pints) of water a day to stay healthy on a desert trek!

Melting arctic ice has uncovered a previously unknown island, now called Warming Island, off the coast of Greenland.

Daintree National Park in Australia is famous for its bouncing stones—they can be bounced off each other like balls! It's said that people who steal the stones get cursed...

Mass extinctions of life on Earth appear to happen about once every 26 million years.

THE EXPLODING BAG

When some materials mix together, it leads to a "chemical reaction." As the materials combine, they change and make something new. In this experiment, you can make gas fill a bag until it pops!

You will need:

- A plastic zip-close bag
- Vinegar
- Baking soda (from the baking section in the supermarket)
- Hot water
- Cup
- Teaspoon
- Toilet paper
- An outdoor area

1 Put about six teaspoons of baking soda on a piece of toilet paper. Fold up the paper around it to make a little package.

2 Outdoors, hold the bag upright. Put in about 125 ml (half a cup) of vinegar and 65 ml (a quarter cup) of hot water.

3 Put the paper package inside the top of the bag. Hold it there while you seal up the opening tightly.

4 Then let the package drop into the vinegar. The vinegar and the baking soda will begin to react.

continues on next page

5

Can you see bubbles of gas forming? How long does it take for the gas to fill up the bag? Don't stand too close—if you're lucky, it will pop!

Another fun idea

What happens if you mix the ingredients in a cup? (Make sure you do this outside, too, or over a sink!)

WHAT HAS HAPPENED?

The baking soda and the vinegar contain different types of chemicals. They react together to make a type of gas called carbon dioxide. The gas spreads out to fill up the bag and pushes against it from the inside.

DID YOU KNOW?

An echo is a sound reflection. To hear an echo, the sound must bounce off a surface that's at least 17 m (56 ft) away. The echo still happens at closer distances, but it comes back too quickly for your ear to hear it.

Recycling one glass bottle saves enough energy to power a computer for 25 minutes.

The *Burj Khalifa* in Dubai, United Arab Emirates, is the world's tallest freestanding building on land measuring 829.8 m (2,722 ft) tall. Not advisable if you're afraid of heights...

In 1896 in a factory in Massachusetts, USA, Dureyas cars became the first mass-produced cars ever made when a run of 13 were built.

The phrase "in the limelight," meaning to be in the public eye, comes from the bright lights used in playhouses before electric lighting was invented. It was made by directing a flame at a cylinder of limestone, which would glow white-hot without burning or melting.

TURN COINS GREEN

Coins such as pennies contain the metal copper. It's normally a pinkish-brown hue—but after being used a lot, these coins turn darker and dirtier. Let's turn them green instead!

You will need:

- Several copper coins (the brownish ones)
- White vinegar
- Salt
- A cup
- A teaspoon
- A shallow bowl
- Paper towel

1 Half-fill the cup with white vinegar, and add a teaspoon of salt. Stir until it disappears.

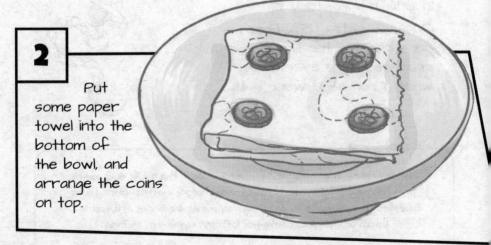

2 Put some paper towel into the bottom of the bowl, and arrange the coins on top.

3

Pour the vinegar mixture over the coins, so they are wet, but not totally covered.

4

Take a few of the coins out, and wash them in water, then leave them to dry on paper towel.

continues on next page

5

Leave the rest of the coins in the vinegar. Add a bit more vinegar if it dries out.

6

After a few hours, compare the two groups of coins. Do they look different?

Another fun idea

Look for bright green roofs and statues when you're out and about. They are made of copper that has reacted with the air.

WHAT HAS HAPPENED?

The salt and vinegar mixture cleans the coins, making them bright and shiny. But those that stay in the vinegar start to turn green! This is because the vinegar helps the copper to react with a gas, oxygen, in the air. This makes a new, green material called copper oxide.

DID YOU KNOW?

Old tales of a rain of blood can be explained by red sand being picked up, carried vast distances in clouds, and falling with the rain.

Water devils are small whirlwinds that make thin columns of water that whirl and twist over the surface of a lake. They can look like the neck of a monster, weaving to and fro, and might explain legends of beasts such as the Loch Ness Monster.

On July 7, 1987, the temperature in Kansas, USA, rose from 24 °C to 35 °C (75 to 95 °F) in just ten minutes!

A lightning bolt is five times hotter than the surface of the Sun.

Only 3 percent of the water on Earth is fresh water—the other 97 percent is salt water in the seas.

There are about 10 million species of living things on Earth.

INVISIBLE INK

Write an invisible secret message that can't be seen. Then use chemical reactions to make it appear! What will your message say?

You will need:

- Paper
- Lemon juice
- A small bowl
- A paintbrush or cotton bud
- A hair dryer or radiator

1 Pour or squeeze your lemon juice into the bowl. Spread out your paper flat to write on.

Try this!

Send a secret essage through the mail to a friend or relative, and ask them to send you one back!

2 Dip your paintbrush or cotton bud in the juice. Use it to write your secret message on the paper (it will be easier if your message is short!).

3 Leave your paper somewhere flat to dry. When dry, give or send it to someone.

Another fun idea

Some other materials can also work as invisible ink. Try apple juice, lemonade, or white vinegar, and see if they work as well.

4 To see the message, the other person needs to heat up the paper. They can leave it on a hot radiator for a while or heat it with a hair dryer. Ta-da! The message is revealed!

WHAT HAS HAPPENED?

Many materials, such as lemon juice, react when they are heated. This makes their appearance change. The juice turns brown as it gets hotter. You can also see this happening when you cook some types of food, such as toast, cake, and onions.

DID YOU KNOW?

The oldest rocks in the world are four billion years old.

The Earth's inner core spins more quickly than the outside. Every 400 years, the inner core makes one complete extra revolution compared to the outside. (Not all in one go—it's just going a bit quicker for the whole 400 years!)

Tornado Alley is an area in the USA, from central Texas to the border of Canada that has the perfect weather conditions for tornadoes.

Some clouds are up to 20,000 m (65,000 ft) thick from top to bottom—nearly three times as tall as the tallest mountain on Earth.

More than 99 percent of Antarctica is covered in snow and ice.

Mount Cotopaxi in Ecuador is on the Equator, usually the hottest area on Earth—but it has a glacier! The mountain is so high that the glacier stays frozen.

If the entire Antarctic ice sheet were to melt, sea levels would rise by 67 m (220 ft), leaving cities such as New York, Hong Kong, and London completely lost under the water.

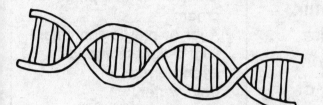

One tenth of the Earth's surface is permanently under ice, and 90 percent of that ice is found in Antarctica.

Escape velocity—the speed you need to travel to escape Earth's gravity is 11.2 km (6.95 miles) per second.

Earthquakes can cause fires when the damage they do breaks electrical or gas lines.

Stinging nettles grow well in soil that contains dead bodies—they thrive on a chemical called phosphorous, which is in the bones.

Areas of Sweden and Finland are still rising as a result of the ice from the last ice age melting. The land rises about 1 m (3.28 ft) in 100 years.

MAKE YOUR OWN BUTTER

Some materials are mixtures and contain two or more things mixed together. Milk and cream are like this. You can't see it, but they're made of tiny pieces of fat mixed into a watery liquid. Can you get them apart?

You will need:

- A carton of whipping cream
- A jar or plastic container with a tight-fitting lid
- Strong arms!
- Cold water
- A bowl or butter dish

1 Leave the carton of cream out of the fridge for a while first. The experiment works best at room temperature.

2 Make sure your container or jar is clean and dry. Pour in the cream and put the lid on tightly.

3 Start shaking! Hold the container or jar firmly, and shake it up and down, up and down.

4 It takes a lot of shaking, so you might need to swap arms or take turns with friends or family.

5 Eventually, you will feel the cream get thicker, then start to make a slapping sound. You'll see it has separated into a lump of butter and a runny, watery liquid called buttermilk.

continues on next page

6 Take the butter out, carefully rinse it in cold water, and put it in a dish. Try it spread on toast!

Another fun idea

If you save the buttermilk that's left behind, you can use it to make pancakes or Irish soda bread. Look in a cookbook for a recipe.

WHAT HAS HAPPENED?

As you shake the cream, the tiny pieces of fat inside it keep banging into each other. Every time they do, they stick together, making bigger and bigger lumps. Finally, they all clump into one lump, separated from the watery liquid (the buttermilk).

DID YOU KNOW?

Planarians are a type of flatworm. They can regenerate (re-grow all their body parts) even from a single, tiny piece. A planarian can grow many heads, and if it's cut up, the little bits make lots of new ones!

An electric eel produces enough electricity to power two refrigerators!

The bombadier beetle produces tiny explosions—up to 500 a second—which blast gases out of its rear end to frighten predators. The exploding farts sound just like a machine gun!

The cusk eel lives more than 8 km (5 miles) below the surface of the sea.

Worms don't chew their food—they swallow small stones, which grind up the leaves and other vegetable matter they eat. Other animals also keep stones in their innards to break up their food—even the dinosaurs did it!

The glass frog is lime green but has a completely transparent stomach. It's possible to see the blood vessels, the heart, and even check whether it's eaten recently or might like a snack.

MAKE SALT CRYSTALS

When you stir salt or sugar into water, it disappears! But it hasn't really gone anywhere. It has dissolved —broken down into tiny parts that are mixed into the water. Some materials can dissolve and then form again as shapes called crystals.

You will need:

- Salt
- Hot water
- A small, heatproof measuring cup
- A teaspoon
- String
- A pencil

1

With an adult to help, half-fill the cup with very hot water or almost-boiling water. Stir in 10 teaspoons of salt.

2

Keep stirring until the salt disappears. Keep adding more salt and stirring, until there is a bit of salt left at the bottom that won't dissolve.

3

Tie a short piece of string to the middle of the pencil. Balance the pencil over the cup, so that the string dangles down into the water.

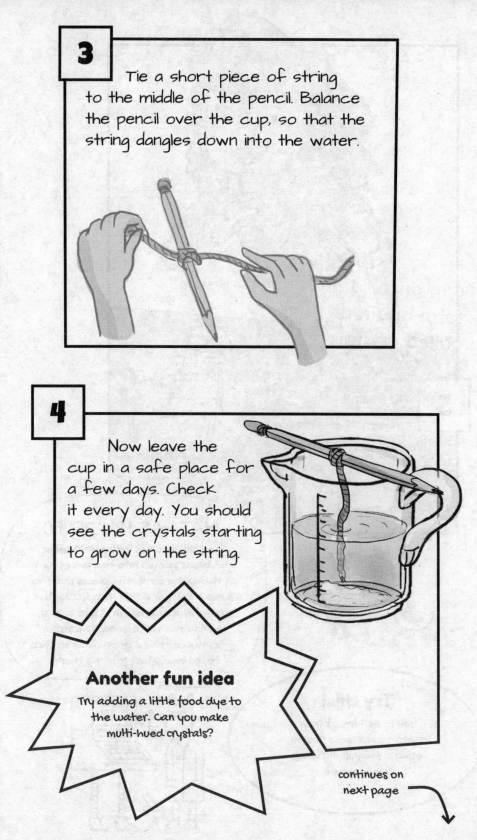

4

Now leave the cup in a safe place for a few days. Check it every day. You should see the crystals starting to grow on the string.

Another fun idea

Try adding a little food dye to the water. Can you make multi-hued crystals?

continues on next page

5 When the string is covered in crystals, you can take it out and look at them closely. Can you see what shape they are?

WHAT HAS HAPPENED?

The salt dissolves in the hot water and breaks down into tiny pieces. But as the water cools, the pieces start to clump together again. Gradually, the water evaporates (turns into a gas), leaving the salt behind. The string gives the crystals a good place to stick to, so they start forming there.

Try this!

You could look at your crystals even more closely, using a magnifying glass or microscope.

DID YOU KNOW?

A quahog clam found off the coast of Iceland was 507 years old, making it the oldest animal ever discovered. The clam was named Ming by researchers, and later renamed Hafrún. It was a baby when Henry VIII was on the throne in England, and was already nearly 300 years old by the time of the French Revolution!

When they eat, planarian worms shoot a tube out of their throats to hold down their prey. They ooze enzymes out to soften the prey and then tear bits off it to eat.

Dragonflies have almost 360 degree vision.

Japanese scientists have bred completely see-through frogs so that they can investigate their internal organs without having to kill and dissect them.

The parasite toxoplasma prefers to live in cats' brains, but it can also infect rats, changing their brains so they are less scared of cats. This makes the rats more likely to be caught and eaten, allowing the parasite to move into the cat!

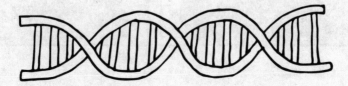

OOBLECK!

Water, milk, and oil are liquids. Rock, plastic, and wood are solids. But oobleck is a little different! It can behave like a solid or a liquid, depending on what you do with it.

You will need:

- A box of cornstarch
- Water
- A plastic bowl
- A measuring cup
- A spoon
- Lots of newspaper to catch the drips!

1

Fill the measuring cup to the brim with water, and pour it into the bowl. Fill the cup with cornstarch, and carefully stir it into the water.

2

Fill the cup with cornstarch again. Stir in more and more, until you have a thick, gloopy mixture (you may need almost all of the second cup).

3 Put the bowl on some newspaper, and play with the oobleck. What happens if you stir slowly? What happens if you try to stir as fast as you can?

Try this!
Change the shade of your oobleck by adding a few drops of food dye to the water at the beginning.

4 Try to grab a handful of oobleck, and squeeze it hard to form a ball. What happens when you let go?

continues on next page

5 Sink your hand into the oobleck, then try to pull it out suddenly. What if you pull it out slowly? You could try the same experiment with a small plastic toy too.

WHAT HAS HAPPENED?

Oobleck is a strange material. When it's pressed hard, the grains of cornstarch lock together, and it can seem solid. When it's handled slowly, it flows and runs like a liquid. There are materials like this in nature, too, such as quicksand.

Tip:
When you're finished, the oobleck can be washed off with warm water.

DID YOU KNOW?

Wildfires travel uphill more quickly than downhill. Hot air rising from the fire dries out the trees on the hillside above it, so they burn more easily.

In 1461 there appeared to be three Suns lined up in the sky over Herefordshire, England. The effect was produced by sundogs—tiny ice crystals in the sky, which reflect light to make ghostly images of the Sun.

According to satellite data, from 2002 through 2019, global tropical forest loss averaged 3.36 million hectares (8.3 million acres) a year —an area larger than Belgium.

The Arctic tundra is a huge, flat, treeless region that has a permanent layer of frost under the ground. The permafrost is 450 m (1,476 ft) deep underground.

The oceans provide 99 percent of the habitable space on Earth because they are so deep—on land, all plant and animal life is clustered on the surface.

The shell of a lobster is made of chitin—the same substance that mushrooms are made of.

ICE TOWER

Many materials freeze, or set hard, as they get cooler—like wax crayons. Normally, when things are frozen, they take up less space. But when water freezes, it gets bigger!

You will need:

- A small plastic water bottle (open)
- Water
- A freezer

1 Fill the bottle all the way up to the top with water.

2 Put it in the freezer (make sure there is a little space above it).

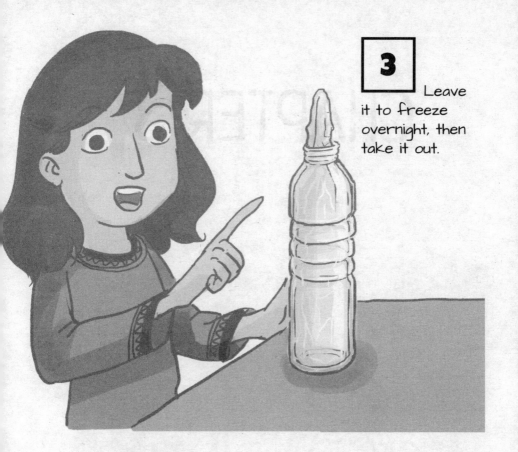

3 Leave it to freeze overnight, then take it out.

WHAT HAS HAPPENED?

As the water freezes, it grows slightly. It has nowhere to go but out of the top of the bottle. It pushes up and forms a "tower" of ice.

Another fun idea
What happens if you freeze a bottle of water and a bottle of sunflower oil, both full to the brim?

CHAPTER 3

Experiments with Energy

ENERGY

Energy is what makes things happen. When things move, heat up, make a noise, or glow with light, it takes energy to make them work. Energy is everywhere—without it, nothing would happen at all!

You take in energy when you eat food and use it to make your body move.

AROUND AND AROUND

Energy does not get "used up." It just changes from one form into another. For example, a candle contains chemical energy. When it burns, the chemical energy turns into heat and light energy.

TYPES OF ENERGY

There are many types, or "forms," of energy. Most of them are things you experience every day. Here are some of the main forms of energy:

Heat: The hotter something is, the more energy is in it.

Light: A form of energy that we can sense with our eyes.

Sound: A form of energy that we can sense with our ears.

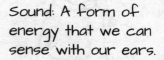

Movement: All movement is a form of energy.

Chemical energy: The energy stored in food and fuel.

Electricity: We use this to power machines.

Try this!

Try these everyday activities to see energy at work.

Turn on a flashlight. It uses electrical energy from the battery to make light glow.

Rub your hands together fast. You put in movement energy, and your hands warm up.

Hit a pan with a wooden spoon. You put in movement energy using your arm. It turns into sound energy.

DID YOU KNOW?

A German aquarium plays love songs to its sharks in an attempt to get them to mate. The technique has also been tried with pandas and monkeys (but not in an aquarium!)

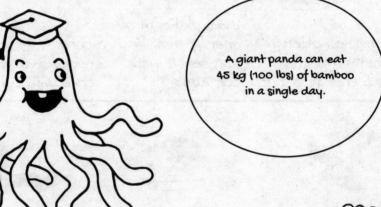

A giant panda can eat 45 kg (100 lbs) of bamboo in a single day.

Tortoiseshell cats are usually female, but if they are born male, they're almost always sterile.

The roots of some pine trees can extend for 48 km (over 30 miles).

The only animals that can recognize their own reflections in a mirror (besides humans) are the great apes, dolphins, and elephants.

Most bacteria are tiny—there can be 50 million bacteria in a single drop of liquid. Yet the largest bacterium can just about be seen with the naked eye.

Swiss vets have found that dogs are suffering from stress more and more. Living in a city and having a demanding owner are two reasons dogs suffer from headaches, stomach pain, and other stress-related symptoms.

In Australia in 2000, a plague of 100 billion locusts attacked wheat and barley crops.

Newts can re-grow body parts that are lost or damaged, including legs, eyes, and even hearts. Scientists who have studied how they do this think they might be able to persuade human bodies to do the same.

Homing pigeons use the Earth's magnetic field to help them find their way home.

HEAT IS MOVEMENT

When things are hot, it actually means they are moving more. These experiments will show you how!

You will need:

- Hot water (not too hot to touch)
- Cold water
- Two glasses
- Three bowls
- Food dye
- Two hands

DISSOLVING DYE

1 Half-fill one glass with hot water and the other with cold water. Stand them side by side.

2 Drip one drop of food dye into each glass. Watch them closely. What happens?

HOT AND COLD

1 Now half-fill one bowl with hot water and another with cold water. Stand them side by side.

2 In the third bowl, mix equal amounts of hot and cold water to make lukewarm water.

3 Put one hand in the hot water and the other in the cold water, and leave them there for one minute.

continues on next page

4

Now take both your hands out, and put them together into the bowl of lukewarm water. How does it feel?

WHAT HAS HAPPENED?

The food dye spreads out faster in the hot water than in the cold water. That's because when the water is warmer, its molecules (the tiny parts it is made of) contain more movement energy. They move faster and push the food dye around.

Colder   Hotter

HOT AND COLD HANDS

When warmer and colder things meet, the movement of the warmer things pushes against the colder things and warms them up. Your hands aren't very good at sensing temperature. Instead, they sense whether they are losing heat energy or getting more. The cold hand is getting more heat energy, so it feels warm. The warm hand is losing heat energy, so it feels cold.

Another fun idea

Instead of food dye, try mixing in sugar. Does it dissolve faster in hot water or cold water?

DID YOU KNOW?

A dog has up to 150 square cm (23.25 square in) of olfactory membrane—the area used to detect smells. A human has around 4 square cm (0.62 square in.).

Armadillos always give birth to quadruplets (four identical babies).

In a rare mutation, chick embryos can grow teeth like crocodiles.

Zebras have individual striped patterns that are as distinctive as fingerprints.

Cows can go upstairs but not downstairs.

The coelacanth is a prehistoric fish which scientists thought had been extinct for 65 million years—until one was found alive and well in 1938!

A rare herb that grows in Bolivia waits 80–150 years before it flowers.

GETTING BIGGER

When things get hotter, the molecules in them move faster. That makes them push away from each other, and they take up more space.

You will need:

- A bag of marshmallows
- A microwaveable plate
- A microwave oven
- A glass bottle
- A coin that covers the opening of the bottle
- A sink with hot and cold faucets

THE MIGHTY MARSHMALLOW

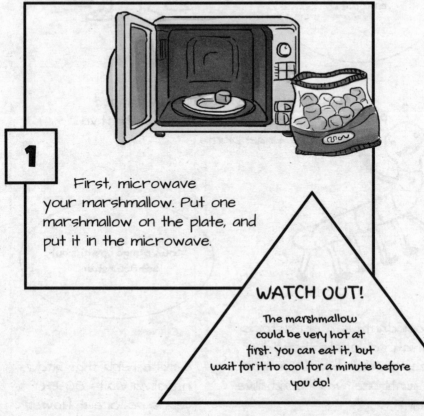

1

First, microwave your marshmallow. Put one marshmallow on the plate, and put it in the microwave.

WATCH OUT!

The marshmallow could be very hot at first. You can eat it, but wait for it to cool for a minute before you do!

2 Turn on the microwave to normal power for 10-15 seconds. Open the door as soon as it stops.

3 Compare the marshmallow with another one from the bag. What's the difference?

BOTTLE BLAST

1 Run cold water into the sink. Put the glass bottle and the coin in to get nice and cold. Then take out the bottle and drain the water from the sink.

2 Empty the bottle, and stand it up. Put the wet coin over the top of it.

continues on next page →

3 Run hot water into the sink to make a shallow bath, and stand the bottle in it. What happens?

WHAT HAS HAPPENED?

Marshmallows contain lots of tiny air bubbles. As they heat up, the molecules in the air move faster and push against each other. The air bubbles get bigger, making the marshmallow grow. The same thing happens inside the bottle. The air warms up and gets bigger. It pushes at the coin on top of the bottle, making it jump.

Another fun idea

What happens if you put a balloon over the neck of the bottle?

DID YOU KNOW?

One comet (a small, tailed object in the Solar System) had its tail ripped off after colliding with a solar storm—ouch!

A radio signal from space, known as the "Wow!" signal, has never been explained and could be real evidence of intelligent life. It was picked up in 1977 and has never been repeated.

The coldest temperature possible is called absolute zero. It is minus 273.15 °C (minus 459.67 °F) and is the temperature at which atoms and molecules stop moving.

Solid waste from space toilets on shuttles is compressed and stored for return to Earth; liquid waste is thrown out into space.

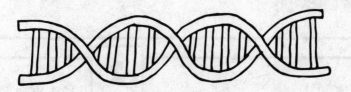

On the International Space Station, all waste from the toilets is stored in a supply craft called The Progress. The craft is eventually released and burns away in Earth's atmosphere.

An astronaut standing on one of Mars' moons would see Mars as a vast red orb—80 times larger than a full moon looks to us.

MAGIC MARBLES

The energy of a moving marble can behave in a strange way!

You will need:

· A medium-size piece of card
· Five marbles or marble-size balls

1 Fold the card in half down the middle, then make two more folds the other way to make a channel, like this.

2 Put your marbles in a row in the channel, like this. They should all be touching each other.

3

Roll one marble back away from the others, then flick it gently toward them. What do you think will happen?

WHAT HAS HAPPENED?

When the moving marble hits the others, they don't all move! Only the one on the other end does. As the first marble hits the second, it passes movement energy into it. The second hits the third, the third hits the fourth, and so on, all passing their energy on. Only the last marble moves, because it has space to.

This toy, called Newton's cradle, works the same way.

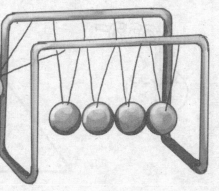

SOUND IS MOVEMENT

How can you make
a balloon buzz?
Try this experiment.

You will need:

- A balloon
- A hexagonal nut
- Lots of breath!

1 Put the
nut inside the
balloon. Blow up
the balloon until
it's fairly big, then
tie it closed.

WATCH OUT!
Keep the nut in the bottom of
the balloon, away from your
mouth, as you blow.

2

Hold the balloon by the top, and move it around in a circle to make the nut whirl around inside. Can you hear a buzz?

WHAT HAS HAPPENED?

Sound is a form of energy that is made when objects vibrate, or move quickly to and fro. As the nut whirls around, its corners bump against the balloon, making it vibrate very quickly. This makes a high buzzing sound!

Another fun idea

Put your hands around the balloon, and hold it up to a working speaker. You'll feel it vibrating!

DID YOU KNOW?

A giraffe can lick inside its own ears.

Sound travels through air at a millionth of the speed of light, which is why you see lightning flash before you hear thunder.

If a cockroach loses a leg, it can grow another!

 Leafcutter ants mix chewed-up leaves with spit and droppings to make yummy compost. They also grow fungus on their compost heaps to eat.

Scientists sometimes pick apart owl pellets (undigested food that owls vomit out) to find out what they've been feeding on. You can even buy owl pellets to examine at home—so get some owl vomit and try it yourself!

 Hydrothermal vents spit scalding-hot steam that is heated underground. Water around one hydrothermal vent near the west coast of the USA can reach 400 °C (752 °F).

A smart toothbrush uses wireless technology to send information to a screen that can be stuck on a bathroom mirror. The toothbrush monitors and reports back on how well you are brushing, and if you've missed any bits!

Crickets hear through their legs.

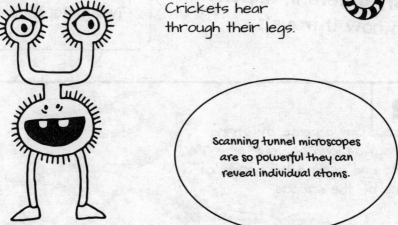

Scanning tunnel microscopes are so powerful they can reveal individual atoms.

People have known that the lead in paint is poisonous since at least 1904—but lead paint was still widely used until the mid-1960s.

Oxygen turns to a blue liquid at minus 183 °C (361 °F). It freezes to a solid at minus 218 °C (424 °F).

Dragonflies can fly at up to 58 km (36 miles) per hour.

Recycling ten drinks cans takes the same amount of energy as making one new one.

SOUND IN A SPOON!

In this experiment, you can find out how the same noise can sound very different, depending on how it travels.

You will need:

- String
- Scissors
- Two metal spoons

1 Cut a piece of string about as long as your arm. Tie one end around the handle of one of the spoons.

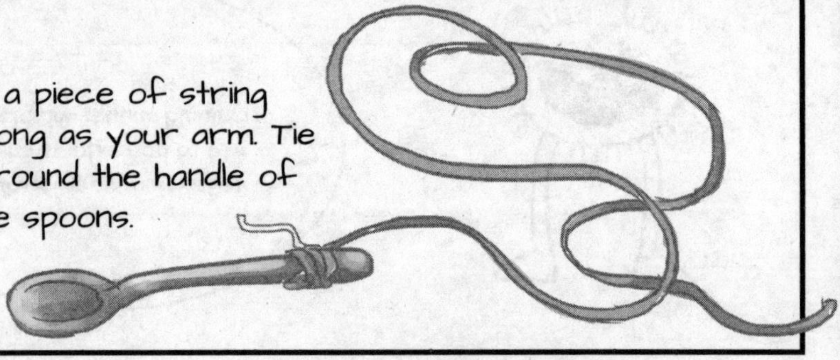

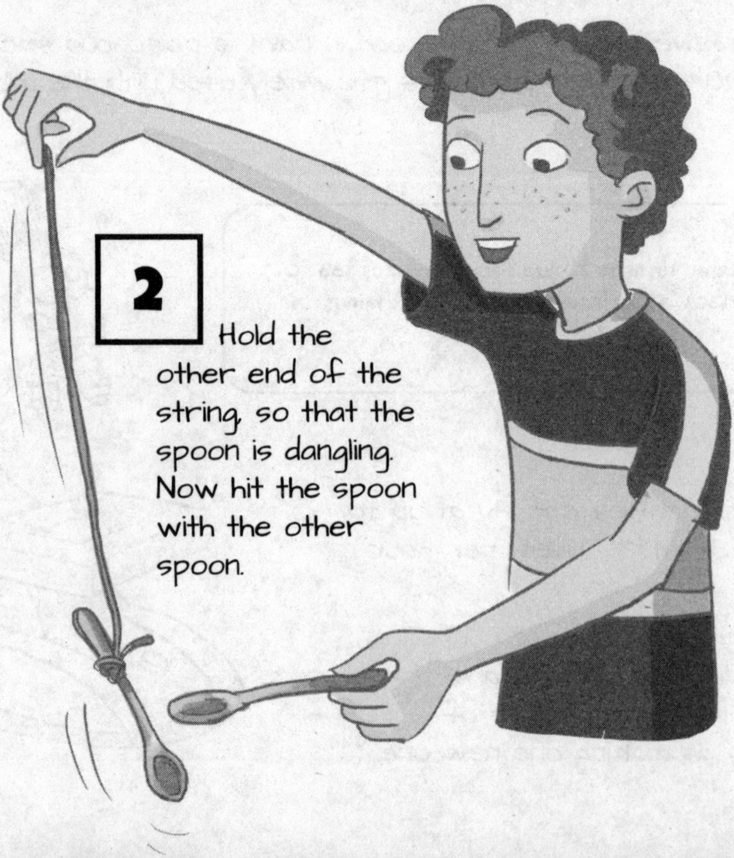

2 Hold the other end of the string, so that the spoon is dangling. Now hit the spoon with the other spoon.

3 What kind of noise does it make? Is it easy to hear? What does it remind you of?

4 Now wrap the end of the string around the tip of your finger, and press your finger against your ear.

WATCH OUT!
Don't stick your finger right inside your ear, since this can be bad for it. Just press it against your ear.

continues on next page

5

Hit the spoon again. Does it sound different? What is different about it?

Another fun idea

Try tying two or more spoons to a longer piece of string. Hold both ends to your ears—or have two people listen to one end each!

WHAT HAS HAPPENED?

Our ears hear sounds because the vibrations that make the sound spread out through the air. The spoon vibrates, it makes the air vibrate, and the vibrations (called sound waves) hit your ears.

But when you press the string against your ear, the sound vibrations spread to your ear along the string, and through your finger and your head. Sound waves travel much faster and better through solid things than they do through air. So this way, the spoon noise sounds louder and stronger.

DID YOU KNOW?

In March 1911, snow that was 11.46 m (37 ft 7 in.) deep fell in California, USA.

The largest nuclear weapon ever tested was the Russian Tsar Bomba, 1961. It had as much energy as a large earthquake, measuring 7 on the Richter scale.

A Hungarian called Ladislo Biro invented the first ballpoint pen in 1938.

The first programmable computer, Colossus, was built in England during World War II to crack coded enemy messages. All 14 Colossus computers were destroyed after the war and the British government denied they had ever existed.

Scientists are trying to make nanoswimmers—tiny devices that can swim through blood vessels to keep people healthy or cure illness.

Soap bubbles blown into air that is below a temperature of minus 15 °C (5 °F) will freeze when they touch a surface. The air inside will gradually diffuse out, causing the bubble to crumple under its own weight.

SEE A SOUND BEFORE YOU HEAR IT

Sound takes time to travel through the air. Light moves much more quickly than sound, and that means you can sometimes see someone making a noise before you hear anything!

1 First, measure a big distance on the ground— 200 m (about 200 yards) is perfect. If it's too hard to measure, just take big steps, counting the number of steps.

29...30!

2 One person stands at one end with the two pots or pans. The other stands at the other end with the stopwatch, ready to start it. You must be able to see each other!

3 The person with the pans should hold them wide apart, then bash them together. At the moment they see the pans touch, the other person should start the stopwatch.

continues on next page →

4

The person with the stopwatch should stop it as soon as they hear the crash of the pans being banged together. How long did the sound take to reach them?

WHAT HAS HAPPENED?

When something makes a sound, the sound vibrations spread out through the air. This means you don't hear sounds right away—it takes a little while for them to travel to you. When you are close to things, it happens quickly and you don't notice it. But when you are far away, you can see something noisy happening but not hear it until a little later.

Try this!

Can you use calculations to figure out how fast the sound was moving?

DID YOU KNOW?

The first mechanical clocks were made in Europe in the thirteenth century. None of the first ones have survived, but they're mentioned in church records from the time.

The Grand Coulee Dam that blocks the Columbia River, USA, is 20 m (66 ft) taller than the Great Pyramid of Egypt.

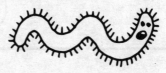

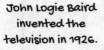

John Logie Baird invented the television in 1926.

Some people think the legendary lost city of Atlantis was on a volcanic island that exploded, destroying the city.

The heaviest building ever to have been relocated while still intact is the Fu Gang Building in the Guangxi Province of China. It weighs 15,140 tonnes (33 million lbs) and is 34 m (111 ft) tall. It was moved a total of 35 m (115 ft) in 11 days.

Electricity doesn't travel through a wire, but in a field around the wire.

MAKE A RAINBOW

Light usually looks white or yellowish. But it is actually made up of all the shades of the rainbow. Here's how to see them.

1

Place the container in bright, direct sunlight (either outdoors or by a window where the Sun is shining in).

2

Pour water into the container until it is as deep as the size of the mirror. Put the mirror into the water.

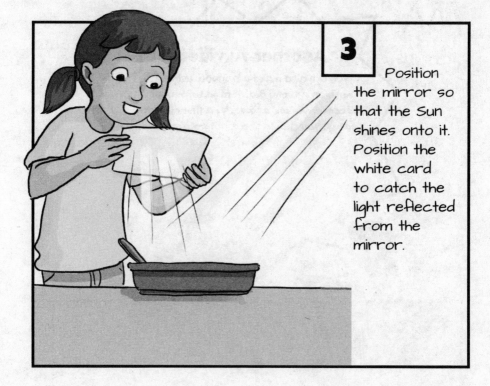

3 Position the mirror so that the Sun shines onto it. Position the white card to catch the light reflected from the mirror.

Gently tilt and move the mirror to get the best position. You should see a rainbow pattern appear on the card.

4

WATCH OUT!
Remember not to look directly at the Sun or at the reflected sunlight—it can damage your eyes.

continues on next page →

Another fun idea

You can also make a rainbow using a hose on a sunny day. Stand with your back to the Sun, and spray a fine mist of water. You should see a rainbow appear in the mist.

WHAT HAS HAPPENED?

White light, like the light that shines from the Sun, is made up of a range, or spectrum, of different hues. When light passes in and out of different see-through substances, such as water or air, it bends, or refracts. The different hues of light bend different amounts. This makes them separate out from each other, and appear as a rainbow.

Scientists use a shaped piece of glass called a prism to split light into its hues.

DID YOU KNOW?

Meghalaya in India has 11,187 mm (467 in.) of rain a year, making it the rainiest place in the world.

More than 10 million bricks were used in the construction of the Empire State Building, New York, USA.

The natural gas burned for heating is methane— the same gas that cows produce when they fart.

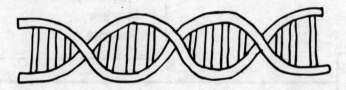

American scientist Selman Waksman studied 10,000 different fungi when looking for a new antibiotic. He eventually found one he needed growing in the throat of a sick chicken.

A bowling pin needs to tilt by a 7.5-degree angle to fall over.

Elephants can't jump.

Putting silver coins in water keeps the water clean. The metal kills bacteria and prevents algae from growing in the water.

The metal gallium melts at body heat—if you held a piece in your hand, it would gradually melt to a liquid pool.

MAKE A PERISCOPE

Light reflects, or bounces, off mirrors. You can use this to help you look around a corner, by making a periscope!

You will need:

- A long cardboard box or container, such as a plastic wrap box
- Two small mirrors that will fit inside the box
- Play clay
- Marker
- Scissors

1 Open the side of the box, so that you can see what you are doing. Some boxes will have a lid that opens, like this.

2 Mark two windows on the box—one at one end of a long side, and one at the other end on the opposite side. Carefully cut them out.

3

Put a large blob of play clay inside the corner opposite each window. Press the blobs into the corners.

4

Press the two mirrors onto the blobs, so that they are positioned diagonally opposite the windows.

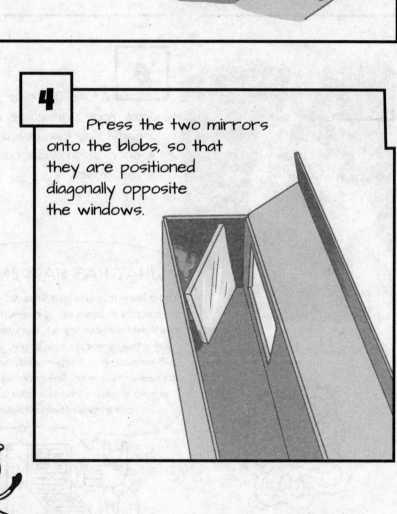

continues on next page

5 You should now be able to look into one window and see out of the other. If you can't, adjust the angles of the mirrors until it works.

6 Close the side of the box. Your periscope is now ready! You can use it to look around a corner or over a wall.

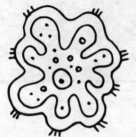

WHAT HAS HAPPENED?

Light travels in straight lines. When it hits a mirror, it bounces off. If the mirror is flat, the light will bounce back the way it came. But if the mirror is at an angle, the light will bounce off in a different direction. The angled mirrors make light coming in at one window bounce along the tube and travel out of the other window.

DID YOU KNOW?

Comets and asteroids are made from the bits and pieces left over from the creation of the Solar System. If someone had tidied up properly, there wouldn't be any!

It is thought that the Moon was formed when a planet collided with Earth and knocked off a huge chunk, about 4.5 billion years ago.

Early astronauts weren't equipped with hot water to rehydrate food, so they ate small, dry cubes of food or meals they squeezed out of tubes.

Some astronauts have suffered from an illness called lunar lung, caused by breathing in moon dust.

The surface of the planet Venus has an average temperature of 480 °C (896 °F). It's unlikely to be the first planet humans visit!

Space toilets have straps for the astronauts' feet and thighs to stop them from drifting off the toilet halfway through!

An early warning system designed to tell us if an asteroid is about to hit the Earth mistook the *Rosetta* spacecraft for a rock that had got dangerously close!

SPARKS IN THE DARK

Light shines from the Sun and stars, lamps, candles, and screens. But there's another, very strange kind of light that can come from things being crushed or ripped.

1

First, set up a dark place. It could be a room with a blackout shade, a dark yard at night, or you could make a dark area under a large blanket.

2

Prepare your experiments with the light on, before taking them into the dark place. Wait in the dark for a few minutes before you start, to help your eyes see the sparks better.

PREPARATION:

Before you go into the dark place that you're going to do your tests in, prepare these things:

1. Stick two strips of tape together, with the ends apart and folded over.
2. Put some sugar cubes in the sandwich bag. Seal it closed.
3. Seal the envelope closed.

TEST 1:

Take the sealed self-seal envelope, and pull open the seal. You may see sparks of light where the glue comes apart.

TEST 2:

Using the pliers, crush the sugar cubes through the bag, and look for flashes of light as they break apart. (Don't pinch your fingers! You might want to get an adult to do this job.)

continues on next page

TEST 3:

Hold the two folded ends of the tape, and rip them apart. Can you see light glowing? Sometimes, pulling tape from the roll can also make light.

WHAT HAS HAPPENED?

This kind of light has a long name—triboluminescence (say try-boe-loo-min-ess-ens). It happens when some types of chemicals break apart.

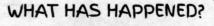

DID YOU KNOW?

In two weeks, the Sun produces as much energy as that stored in all the coal, gas, and petroleum reserves that there have ever been on Earth!

Copepods (tiny crustaceans) often live in groups of up to a trillion (1,000,000,000,000).

In space, all liquids (including urine) simultaneously boil and freeze. A liquid that is spilled or dumped into outer space instantly spreads out into the surrounding air, then the droplets freeze into a fine haze of ice crystals.

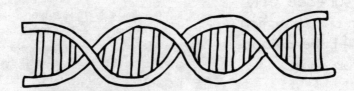

A light year is the distance that light can travel in one year. It works out at about 10 million km (6 million miles)!

The South African quiver tree cuts its own branches off to preserve water. Clever tree!

Astronauts have to spend time in quarantine before and after they go into space.

STATIC ELECTRIC GAMES

Electricity is a form of energy. One type of electricity is called static. It can build up in objects and make them behave in weird ways.

You will need:

- Balloons
- A wool sweater, blanket, or scarf
- A wall
- Tissue paper
- Empty soda cans

TO START WITH ...

Rub the balloon several times on the wool surface. Only rub in one direction, then lift the balloon and rub again.

Another fun idea

You can also rub a plastic object, such as a comb or a ruler, to give it an electric charge. See if it can pick up the tissue paper.

138

ON THE WALL

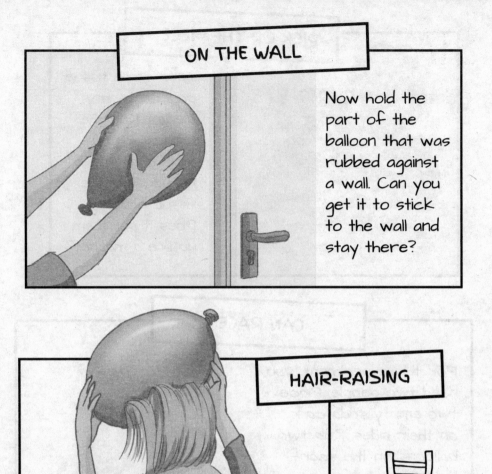

Now hold the part of the balloon that was rubbed against a wall. Can you get it to stick to the wall and stay there?

HAIR-RAISING

Rub the balloon on your hair. Then slowly lift the balloon up ... and it should pull your hair up with it!

continues on next page →

PICK UP THE PIECES

Tear some tissue paper into tiny pieces. Rub the balloon on the wool again, then hold it over the tissue paper. Does it pull them up like a magnet?

CAN RACE

For this experiment, you need two people. Place two empty soda cans on their sides. Rub two balloons on the scarf. Hold the balloons near the cans, and they will start to roll. Who can make theirs go fastest?

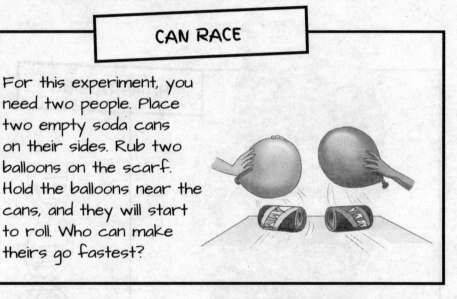

WHAT HAS HAPPENED?

Objects contain tiny parts called electrons, which can move. Moving electrons make electricity. When you rub the balloon on the wool, some electrons move from the wool into the balloon. This makes an electrical pull, or charge, between the balloon and other objects.

DID YOU KNOW?

Phosphorus (the chemical used for making matches) was first created when chemists extracted it from their urine. The urine was left to stand until it putrefied (went bad). It was later extracted from burned and crushed bones.

Two billion atoms would fit on the dot of this i.

The first computers used to be so big that they would take up a whole room! By the 1960s the electronic parts were getting smaller, so they gradually shrank in size. Today, computers can be so tiny they can fit inside your hand!

Archeologists have found what they think was a cream for treating pimples in the tomb of an ancient Egyptian prince.

Wormholes (if they exist) are tunnels through space and time, which could possibly be used for time travel.

There are now robots that are so life-like that they can copy human expressions like smiling, sneering, frowning, and squinting.

THE BROKEN STRAW

How can a straw be whole but look as if it's in two pieces? All you need is water.

You will need:

- A glass
- A straw
- Water

1

Fill the glass with water almost to the top.

2

Put the straw into the water, so that it leans over sideways.

3

Look at the straw from the side. What has happened to it?

WHAT HAS HAPPENED?

The straw is just the same as it always was, but it looks different. This is because of refraction——the way light bends when it passes in or out of something see-through. Part of the straw is in the air, and the light from it comes straight to your eyes. Part of it is in the water, and the light from it bends as it moves through water and glass on its way to you. So the two parts look as if they are in different places.

Did you know?

Objects like straws don't shine with light. But you see them because light from the sun, or a lamp, bounces off them and enters your eyes.

DID YOU KNOW?

Nuttall's poorwill is an American bird that hibernates in the winter, hiding in a crack in a rock. During this time, it uses only a thirtieth of the energy it uses in the summer and its heartbeat becomes so faint that it can't be felt.

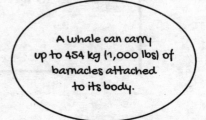

A whale can carry up to 454 kg (1,000 lbs) of barnacles attached to its body.

Early European explorers thought that a giraffe was a cross between a camel and a leopard and called it "cameleopard!"

A Galapagos tortoise called Harriet (said to have been collected by Charles Darwin in 1835) lived at a zoo in Brisbane, Australia, until she died in 2006—making her over 170 years old!

The Arctic tern flies a round trip of 35,000 km (21,750 miles) a year, breeding in the Arctic in the northern summer and feeding in the Antarctic during the southern summer.

When they are young, flatfish look like ordinary fish with an eye on each side. As they grow, one eye moves around so that both eyes are on the same side! The fish becomes wider and flatter and begins to live lying flat at the bottom of the sea.

The male anglerfish is much smaller than the female and spends most of his life attached to his mate's body. That's one way to make sure to stay together forever!

A hippopotamus has skin that's 3.5 cm (1.5 in.) thick—it's almost bulletproof!

The sooty tern can stay airborne for 10 years. It eats, drinks, and sleeps while flying, and only lands to breed and rear its young.

Any magnetic material that is touching a magnet starts to behave like a magnet, too! If you attach a paper clip to a magnet you'll discover that you can attach another one to the first paper clip ... then another... as many as you like! If you then break the first clip's contact with the real magnet, they will all fall off and lose their "stolen" magnetism!

There are 8,000 small earthquakes (measuring less than 2 on the Richter scale) each day—they are too small for people to even feel them.

The International Space Station is equipped with huge solar panels and all its power comes from the Sun.

Moths, butterflies, beetles, and mites eat the various algae that grow on a sloth.

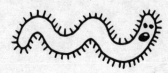

CHAPTER 4

Experiments
with Living Things

LIVING THINGS

What makes you different from a coin, a spoon, or a chunk of ice? You're alive—an eating, breathing, growing, living thing. Our world is full of living things, from humans like you to huge whales, trees and flowers, dogs and cats, insects, and tiny germs.

WHAT ARE LIVING THINGS?

There are millions of types of living things, and they are all different. But there are some things that all living things do ...

THEY MOVE ...

Plants lean toward the Sun.

People walk, run, or dance.

THEY FEED ...

Lions eat antelopes.

This toadstool feeds on a rotting tree stump.

THEY SENSE ...

Plants sense light.

A shark sniffs out its prey.

THEY GROW ...

You grow as you get older.

A sunflower grows very tall.

THEY MAKE MORE LIVING THINGS!

Birds lay eggs.

These bacteria are splitting in two to make more bacteria.

Babies are born.

WHICH IS WHICH?

The types of living things are called species. Each species is different and has its own name. The species can be divided into larger groups.

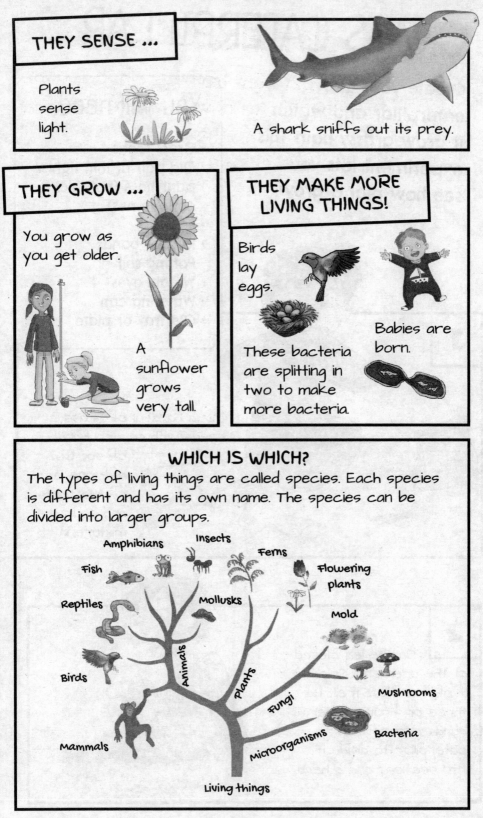

Amphibians
Insects
Ferns
Fish
Flowering plants
Reptiles
Mollusks
Mold
Animals
Plants
Birds
Mushrooms
Fungi
Mammals
Microorganisms
Bacteria
Living things

GRASS CATERPILLAR

Create your own caterpillar and watch it grow grassy hair! This experiment lets you see how plants grow.

You will need:

- Grass seeds
- Old pair of thin tights/ pantyhose (not thick cotton ones)
- Scissors
- Rubber bands
- Potting soil
- Wiggle eyes
- Watering can
- Old tray or plate

1

Mix a handful of grass seeds with several handfuls of soil. Cut off one leg of the tights and pour the mixture in.

2 Tie the leg closed at the open end. Snip it off neatly. Stretch three or four rubber bands around the caterpillar to divide it into sections and a head.

3 Stick some wiggle eyes on the head (or make your own using buttons). Put the caterpillar on a tray or plate.

4 Put the tray or plate with your caterpillar on it on a sunny windowsill. If it's spring or summer, it could go outside if you have space.

continues on next page →

5 Water your caterpillar's body every day, making sure it stays damp. Soon, its hair will start to appear! How long does it take to grow?

WHAT HAS HAPPENED?

When the grass seeds have plenty of light, water, and soil, they start to grow. They grow roots and long leaves, which look like furry hair.

Another fun idea

What happens if you make a caterpillar but leave it somewhere dark? What happens if you don't water it? Try these tests to see what conditions seeds need to grow properly.

DID YOU KNOW?

In 1945, crocodiles killed 980 Japanese soldiers (of 1,000 in total) who entered a mangrove swamp to escape the British navy.

Some scientists believe that hidden or "silent" genes can return after millions of years. A "throw back" happens if a silent gene gets turned back on—making dolphins with legs, for example, or people who are as hairy as apes!

The killifish lives in temporary ponds in Venezuela. When the ponds dry up, the killifish embryos can survive in the mud, with no water or oxygen, for more than 60 days. No other creature can hold its breath for so long!

A rhino's rock-solid horn is made of keratin—the same substance as human hair, skin, and nails.

Shaving a pregnant mouse makes her produce more milk and grow larger babies. A bald mouse can digest more food without overheating, and so makes more milk.

The cosmopolitan sailfish can swim faster than a cheetah can run! It can swim at least 109 km (68 miles) per hour, while a cheetah can only manage 100 km (62 miles) per hour.

RAINBOW CELERY

Have you ever seen a plant with red or blue leaves? Here's a clever way to make a stick of celery change its hue. It will look like magic!

You will need:

- Sticks of celery with leaves
- Two small glasses
- Red and blue food dye
- Water
- Kitchen scissors

1

Trim the bottom of a stick of celery, so that it is about 15 cm (6 in) long. Leave the leaves on.

2

Pour water into a glass, so that it is a third full. Add a little bit of food dye.

3 Put the end of the celery into the liquid in the glass. Leave the glass in a safe place, where it won't be moved.

4

After one day, cut across the base of the celery with scissors. You will see lines of dye rising up the stalk.

6

On the following day, you will have rainbow celery! Cut back the stalks to check.

5 Put water and a small amount of a different food dye in each of two glasses. Split another stick of celery. Allow each part of the split stalk to stand in a glass.

WHAT HAS HAPPENED?

Plants need water, just like we do. They take up water through their roots. The water travels in little tubes, all the way through the stem to the leaves. If you put dye in the water, the dye will be carried to the leaves, too!

DID YOU KNOW?

A mushroom from Africa, called the Lady in the Veil, grows faster than any other organism in the world. It grows up to 20 cm (8 in.) in only 20 minutes, and can be heard cracking as it grows!

Trees grow from their tops——so if you carve your name into a tree when you (and the tree) are small it will still be at the same height when you are old.

Some trees communicate using chemicals. If a wood-eating bug attacks one, the tree releases chemicals into the air, which prompt other trees in the area to produce a poison that deters the bugs.

There have been rainstorms with falling fish, frogs, and toads!

In 1894, a turtle that was frozen inside a giant hailstone fell to Earth.

Rain forests cover a mere 2 percent of the Earth, yet more than half of all plant and animal species live there.

Some types of plants and animals have evolved to live in the most hostile places, such as inside volcanic vents, at the bottom of vast caves, and even deep under the sea.

Scientists working in the rain forests often find their feet go green and slimy. Fungi, which usually break down old leaves on the forest floor, are just as happy living on a wet, smelly foot.

The expression "once in a blue Moon" means that something hardly ever happens. A blue Moon does happen occasionally though—it happened in 1950 when a large wildfire in Canada sent soot high up into the sky, making the Moon look blue.

Hot water freezes more quickly than cold water.

A peanut is not really a nut—it grows underground!

Lake Titicaca in Bolivia is home to lots of sea creatures—but it's an inland lake. The lake was stranded when the landscape changed, trapping sea creatures in its saltwater environment.

There is not always thunder with lightning.

Some cold-water coral reefs have been growing since the end of the last ice age—10,000 years ago.

157

DRIED FRUIT

There's one thing that all living things need, and that's water. In this experiment, you can find out just how watery plants are.

You will need:

- A selection of fruit, such as an orange, an apple, a peach, and a banana
- A knife
- An oven
- A baking sheet
- Food scale
- Pencil and paper
- An adult to help

1

Weigh each fruit, and write down how much it weighs. Then slice up each fruit thinly. Spread the slices out on the baking sheet.

2

With an adult's help, put the sheet in the oven. Set it to the lowest heat—usually about 100 °C (225 °F). Leave it for about 6 hours, then switch the oven off and leave it overnight to cool.

3

Once cool, carefully take out the sheet of dried-out fruit. Weigh each fruit again. How much less does each weigh?

WHAT HAS HAPPENED?

Living things are made of tiny units called cells. Cells need water to make them work. Plants also take in water in order to make food and grow. A typical fruit is over 80 percent (or four-fifths) water. A human is a little bit less watery—around 60–70 percent..

FLOWER PHOTOS

Take a series of flower photos to see how a flower opens its petals and blooms. You'll need to start in the morning—it could take the whole day!

1

Stand your flower in the vase or pitcher of water. Set up your camera pointing at the flower. If you don't have a tripod, use model clay to hold it still.

2

Take a photo of the flower every 20 or 30 minutes. Make sure you keep the lights on all day, so it is easy to see.

3

Once the flower has opened, upload all your photos onto a computer. Arrange them in order of the time they were taken.

WHAT HAS HAPPENED?

It's hard to see a flower opening, since it moves so slowly. But your photos let you see how it happens.

DID YOU KNOW?

A "doomsday vault" has been built in an Arctic cave to store seeds from all the world's food-giving plants in case a major disaster wipes them all out. It contains 4.5 million seed samples that will be able to survive for up to 1,000 years.

All the animals on Earth combined use 10,000 tonnes (over 22 million lbs) of oxygen a second.

In 90 percent of avalanche accidents, the snow fall is triggered by a human being.

The twin-spurred pitcher plant is also home to ants that eat some of the insects that fall in. The plant doesn't mind; the ants break up the insects, making them easier for the meat-eating plant to digest.

A black hole is an area in space with a gravitational field that is so strong, that nothing inside it can ever escape—not even light—which is how they got their rather dark name ...

Over 99 percent of all the species in the world that have ever lived are already extinct!

Inside the vents of active volcanoes, bacteria live in conditions equivalent to a vat of hydrochloric acid. They're not fussy about their homes!

When polar ice melts, it sometimes reveals woolly mammoths frozen since the end of the last ice age. The mammoth meat can still be fresh—on one occasion, dogs ate the defrosted mammoth before scientists could investigate it!

The gigantic dinosaur Sauroposeidon could stretch its neck up to 17 m (55 ft).

The South American stinkhorn fungus smells of rotten meat and old toilets, and has a slimy white spike which is irresistible to flies. Not a good pot-plant for your bedroom!

Some trees can live for a very long time. A redwood tree which fell over in California, USA, in 1977 is thought to have been 6,200 years old—which means it started to grow 2,000 years before the earliest human civilizations started.

In the 1700s a Russian woman had 69 children: 16 pairs of twins, 7 sets of triplets, and 4 sets of quadruplets. That's a lot of birthdays to remember!

Penguins can't fly, but they can jump nearly 2 m (6 ft) into the air.

Brazil nut trees grow happily in the rain forest environment and refuse to grow anywhere else in the world. Scientists have tried to remove them to cultivate in labs, but the trees don't like it.

When you look at your tongue first thing in the morning, it is covered in white stuff. These are cells that died during the night.

THE RUBBERY BONE

Bones are hard—aren't they? They hold your body up and protect soft parts, like your brain. But you can make a bone go bendy and rubbery. Here's how!

You will need:

- A cooked chicken bone
- A plastic food container with a lid
- White vinegar
- Paper towel

1 First, you'll need to get your bone. The best way is to pull apart a well-cooked chicken leg. Take the bone out, and wash it well.

2 Put the bone in the container, then pour in enough white vinegar to cover it completely. Put the lid on tightly.

3 Leave the container somewhere safe for at least five days. Then open it, take the bone out, wash it, and dry it with a paper towel.

4 You'll find the bone has become rubbery and soft! Can you bend it in half? Can you tie a knot in it?

Did you know?

Dairy products like milk and cheese contain calcium. That's why they are good for helping your body to grow strong bones and teeth. If you can't eat dairy foods, though, you can also get it from leafy vegetables like cabbage, or from beans, sardines, oranges, and nuts.

Try this!

Can you feel some of the hard bones in your body? Try feeling your head, cheeks, ankles, and knees.

WHAT HAS HAPPENED?

Animal bones—including your own—contain a mineral called calcium. It is what makes bones hard and strong. Vinegar is good at dissolving calcium. When it soaks into the bone, the calcium dissolves. The softer, bendy parts of the bone are left behind.

= Calcium

Bone soaking in vinegar

DID YOU KNOW?

Some plants grow faster if they are played music. Researchers found the most effective music was "Bat out of Hell" by the singer Meatloaf!

The smallest type of tree is a dwarf willow that grows in Greenland. It is only 5 cm (2 in.) tall.

Cyanide is a poison that can be made from several plants. A tiny amount is deadly in just five minutes.

If a chicken is caught up in a tornado, its feathers can be ripped out—but it can still survive.

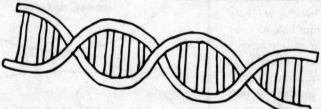

Some plants, including grass, produce a poison when something starts to eat them. This is a chemical response to protect the rest of the plant.

The lily pads of a giant water lily that grows in the Amazon are strong enough for a small child to sit on.

The taste of rat poison varies in different countries. It is adapted to suit the food rats are most used to.

A book of plants published in England in 1597 claimed that tomatoes are poisonous. The author acknowledged that they were eaten regularly in Spain and Italy, though!

A puffball fungus can release 7 billion spores in a single day. Luckily, they don't all grow, or there would be fungi everywhere you looked!

Many animals, including foxes, squirrels, cockroaches, and mice, have adapted to urban living. Cities aren't their natural habitat, but there's lots of food and it's nice and warm—why would they ever leave?!

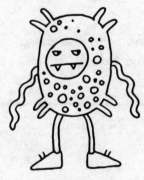

Some desert plants have adapted to their dry environment by growing really long roots that suck water from deep underground.

Some fungi glow in the dark and can be seen from 15 m (50 ft) away. They are used as natural lanterns.

When girls are one and a half years old, they are almost half their adult height. The same happens for boys when they are two.

The seeds of the orchid flower are so light that just over 1 million of them weigh only 1 g (0.035 oz).

FLY-EYE GLASSES

Lots of animals have eyes. They use them to sense light, which helps them to tell where objects are. But not all eyes are the same. Make these glasses, and see the world through a fly's eyes!

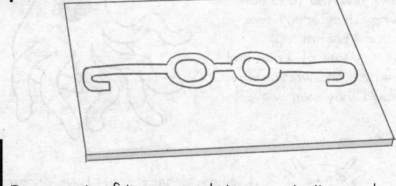

1

Draw a pair of large, round glasses onto the card, like this. Include the arms sticking out at the sides.

2

Carefully cut out your glasses, including the holes for the eyes. Fold the arms inward, then check that your glasses fit you.

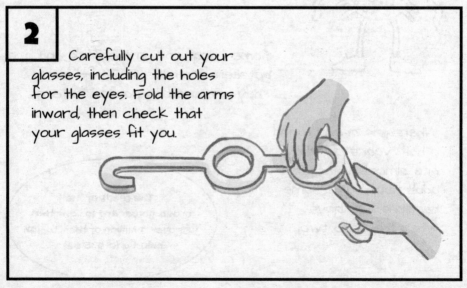

3

On the bubble wrap, draw two circles the same size as the frames of your glasses. Cut them out.

4

Glue or tape the bubble wrap circles to the inside of your glasses frames. Once they are firmly in place, try on your glasses!

WHAT HAS HAPPENED?

Flies and many other insects have special eyes called compound eyes. They are made up of lots of mini eyes, all tightly packed together. The fly sees an image of the world divided into small sections—like looking through bubble wrap.

Another fun idea

With the glasses off, try covering one eye and looking around. Do things look different? Your two eyes give you two slightly different views of the world. This lets you see in 3D and judge how far away things are.

Try this!

If you can catch a fly in a glass, try looking at it closely. Use a magnifying glass, if you have one. Can you see its compound eyes?

DID YOU KNOW?

Mitochondria are parts of the cells in our bodies. Scientists think that they were originally bacteria, which have become absorbed into our bodies and are now an essential part of us. They take in nutrients and make energy for our cells.

The skin of your eyelid is only 0.5 mm (0.02 in) thick, the same width as a single hair.

A lightning bolt is around 7.6 cm (3 in.) wide and 3.2 km (2 miles) long.

Some substances change the appearance of your urine—if you eat lots of rhubarb, your urine will be orange, and blackberries can make it go red!

Most people's ears grow 0.25 mm (0.01 in.) per year for their whole life.

There are 100 billion stars in a typical galaxy.

Every day, you produce enough saliva in your mouth to fill five cups.

In 1804, trainee doctor Stubbins Firth tried to prove that yellow fever is not an infectious disease by drinking his patients' vomit! Although he did not get yellow fever, he was wrong. It is very contagious, but must enter directly through the bloodstream.

The skeleton of a body buried in pH-neutral soil or sand can survive for thousands of years.

Carrots really do help you see in the dark—they contain vitamin A, which helps the retina to develop.

If you mix corn syrup and tar together by stirring, you can separate them again by stirring in the opposite direction.

A traditional treatment for the pain of arthritis is bee venom ... but then you're faced with the pain of bee stings!

Even when you are elderly, you will still have the tooth enamel that was formed in your mother's womb.

The amount of electrical energy generated by your brain is enough to power a light bulb!

GROWING DOUGH

Cut a slice of bread, and you'll see it's full of bubbles. But did you know what makes those bubbles? The answer is tiny living things.

You will need:

- 450 g (1 lb) bread flour
- 1 teaspoon of dried yeast
- 1 teaspoon of salt
- 1 teaspoon of sugar
- Olive oil
- 300 ml (1¼ cups) of warm water
- A mixing bowl
- Plastic wrap
- A baking sheet
- An adult to help

1

Put the flour, yeast, and salt in the bowl. Mix the sugar and 1 tablespoon of oil into the water, then add the water to the flour. Use your hands to mix it together.

2

Shape and squeeze the ingredients to make a soft dough. Tip it out onto a table sprinkled with flour, and knead it for 5 minutes.

3

Oil the baking sheet, and put your dough on it. Oil the top of the dough, then spread a piece of plastic wrap over it. Leave it in a warm place for an hour.

4

After an hour, the dough should be much bigger! Now get ready to bake it in the oven to make bread.

Tip!

Here's how to knead: Fold the dough in half. Press it down with both hands. Stretch it out a little sideways. Fold in half again ... and keep going!

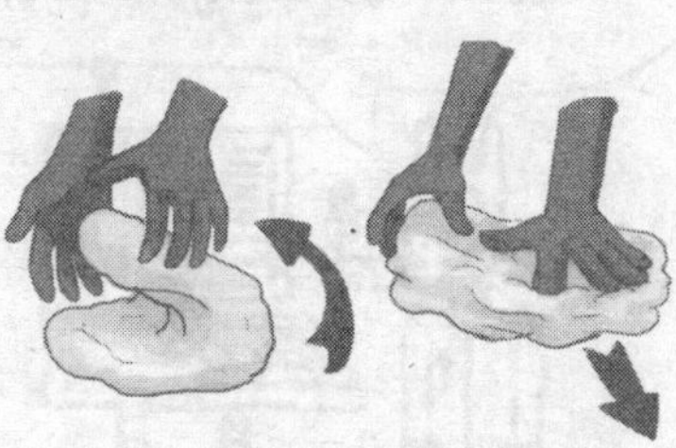

continues on next page

5 Remove the plastic wrap. Preheat the oven to 200 °C (400 °F). With an adult's help, put the bread dough in the oven and bake it for 30–35 minutes.

6 Carefully take the baked bread out, and leave to cool. When it's ready, cut a slice and look at the bubbles inside.

WHAT HAS HAPPENED?

Yeast is actually a living thing. It is a type of fungus that is related to mushrooms. When it has water, warmth, and a supply of sugar, it starts to feed. As it feeds, it makes bubbles of gas. The bubbles make the dough "rise" and get bigger.

Another fun idea

You can make bread dough into shapes before leaving them to rise. (They will need less baking time— about 10 minutes.)

DID YOU KNOW?

Plants often grow inside the skeletons of dead bodies in the Arctic—they make warm homes and have lots of nutrients that nourish plants.

Window plants in the Namib Desert grow transparent crystals on their leaves to protect them from the hot Sun.

Some explorers have drunk the juice inside pitcher plants—a mixture of the plant's acidic digestive juices and its half-dissolved victims. Yum!

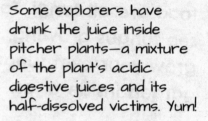

The largest bacteria are 1 mm (0.039 in) long and are big enough to see with the naked eye.

A pinch of soil holds 5 billion bacteria—nearly enough for everyone on the planet to have one each!

The pink petticoat plant has a flower that looks like a pretty skirt—it might look nice but it gobbles up bugs that crawl inside it.

The saguaro cactus has a woody skeleton inside it! Some animals live in the skeleton once the plant has died.

FUNGUS GARDEN

A fungus (more than one fungus = fungi) is a kind of living thing. Yeast, mushrooms, and the furry or slimy stuff that grows on old food are all fungi. To see fungus growing, grow your own fungus garden inside a jar.

You will need:

- Old fruit, old cheese, and stale bread, cake, or cookies
- A knife
- A glass jar with a tight-fitting lid
- Tape
- Water
- Pen and label

1

Chop up your food items into chunks. Sprinkle each one with water, and put them inside the jar.

2

Screw on the lid tightly. Then wrap tape around the edge of the lid, too, for an extra-tight seal.

3 Write "Fungus Garden —do not open!" on your label, then stick it on the jar.

4 Put the jar in a safe place where no one will throw it away or play with it.

continues on next page →

5

Check the jar every day. You should see furry fungi starting to grow on the food.

Try this!

Try looking more closely at the fungi with a magnifying glass. Can you see different types of fungus? Can you see little stalks or hairlike parts?

WHAT HAS HAPPENED?

Spores

Fungi grow hairs, like tiny roots, into the food to feed on it.

Like mushrooms and toadstools, fungi release tiny spores into the air. The spores work like seeds. If they land on food, they can start to grow into new fungi. As food starts to get old, fungi collect and grows on it.

When you're finished with the experiment, throw the jar away, unopened. Fungi can be bad for you—it's best not to let it escape.

DID YOU KNOW?

The Australian bloodwood tree oozes red sap that looks like blood when it is cut.

The anacampseros plant looks like a bird dropping to protect it from being eaten by animals.

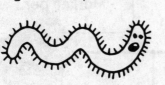

A pumpkin can grow roots with a total length of 24 km (15 miles).

Avalanches kill over 150 people worldwide every year. They are mostly skiers and snowboarders.

Genetic engineering can combine genes from different plants and animals. A gene from a deep sea fish can be added to a vegetable to make it frost resistant! Some people call genetically modified foods like this "Frankenstein foods."

Scientists believe 70 percent of dinosaurs are yet to be discovered, as more new species have been found in the last 20 years than ever before.

SPINNING PICTURES

It is easy for your eyes to get confused. If you see things spinning very quickly, they can seem to blend together into one.

1

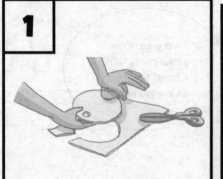

Cut out a circle of card 8 cm (3 in) across. Make a hole on each side with the hole punch.

2

Cut two pieces of string, then thread one through each hole. Tie each string in a knot to hold it in place.

3

Draw a picture, such as a goldfish, in the middle of the card. Flip this over, so that it's upside down.

4

Draw another picture on the other side to go with the first picture, such as a goldfish bowl.

5

Hold the strings on either side of the card, close to the holes. Twist your fingers to make the picture spin over and over.

Another fun idea

Here are some more ideas for pictures. Can you think of others, too?

6

As you watch the picture spinning, can you see the two pictures appear as one image?

WHAT HAS HAPPENED?

Your eyes work by detecting patterns of light and sending signals to your brain. When you see an image, it lasts for a little while in your brain, even if it has disappeared in real life. The spinning picture moves so fast that both images end up in your brain at the same time, and they seem to get mixed together.

Did you know?

This experiment was invented more than 150 years ago. In the 1800s, it was called the "thaumatrope."

GRABBING HAND

Reach out your hand, and pretend to grab something. Your fingers curl up toward each other. How do they do that? Find out with this model hand.

You will need:

- Card
- Pens
- Scissors
- Straws
- Tape
- String

1 Draw around your hand and wrist onto the card. Cut the shape out using the scissors, and decorate it with pens or pencils.

2 On the hand, mark each finger into three sections, like real fingers. Fold the fingers between the sections, like this.

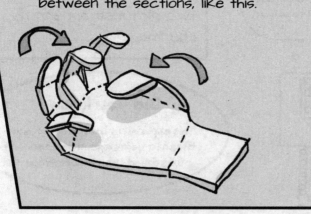

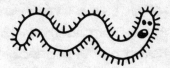

3

Cut pieces of straw slightly shorter than each finger section. Tape the pieces of straw onto the fingers, so that they line up.

4

Tape longer pieces of straw onto the palm of the hand, leading from each finger to the wrist. Make sure they all end at the same place.

continues on next page

5

Cut five long pieces of string. Thread them through the straws for each finger, and tape them in place at the fingertips.

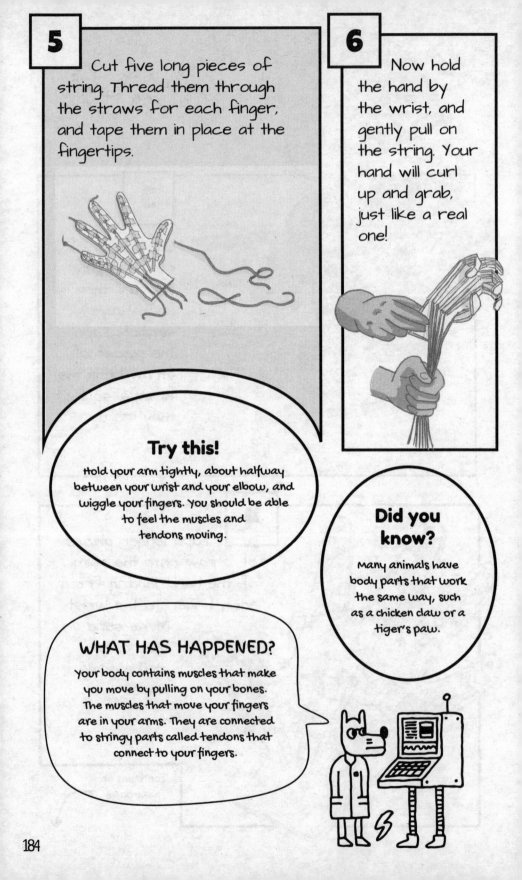

6

Now hold the hand by the wrist, and gently pull on the string. Your hand will curl up and grab, just like a real one!

Try this!

Hold your arm tightly, about halfway between your wrist and your elbow, and wiggle your fingers. You should be able to feel the muscles and tendons moving.

Did you know?

Many animals have body parts that work the same way, such as a chicken claw or a tiger's paw.

WHAT HAS HAPPENED?

Your body contains muscles that make you move by pulling on your bones. The muscles that move your fingers are in your arms. They are connected to stringy parts called tendons that connect to your fingers.

DID YOU KNOW?

Being born with webbed hands or feet is quite common. It happens because fingers and toes develop from a flipper-like hand or foot that divides on the unborn baby. If it doesn't divide properly, the skin stays webbed.

It's possible that hiccups come from our distant ancestors who crawled out of swamps and had both lungs and gills. Hiccups may be a remnant of a way of closing off their lungs when in the water.

Most human mutations happen on the Y chromosome, which only men have.

Sound travels faster in warm air than in cold air.

Your skin weighs about 3 kg (6.5 lbs) — the same as a bag of potatoes.

A man born in England long ago had four eyes, arranged one pair above the other. He could close any one eye independently of the others.

BLINK REFLEX

A reflex is something your body does by itself, without you deciding to do it. Reflexes can be useful, since they help to protect us.

You will need:

- A door with a glass window in it
- Cotton balls
- Two or more people

1 One person should stand behind the glass, with their face up close to it and their eyes wide open.

2 Another person should stand on the other side of the glass, and throw cotton balls at the first person's face, one at a time.

3 The first person has to try not to blink. When they've taken a turn, swap places. It's very hard to keep your eyes open!

WHAT HAS HAPPENED?

Your blink reflex makes your eyes shut if anything moves quickly toward your face. Even though you know the glass is in the way, it's very hard to stop your eyes from shutting.

Did you know?

Your blink reflex protects your eyes from dangers such as flying sand or insects.

FOOD TUBES

When you eat food, it goes into your stomach, then travels through a long set of tubes called intestines. Let's find out how long they are!

You will need:

- A tape measure
- A ball of string
- Pen and paper
- A calculator
- At least two people

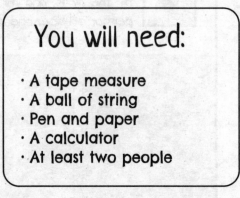

1 First, ask someone to measure how tall you are. Write down the results on your paper.

130 cm
(51 in)

2 Use the calculator to multiply your height by five. Write down the answer on the paper.

130 cm
(51 in)
x 5 =

3 The answer shows how long your intestines are! Measure out a piece of string that long.

WHAT HAS HAPPENED?

You have two intestines—the small intestine and the large intestine. The small intestine soaks up food chemicals into your body. Its length is about four times your height. The large intestine collects waste and turns it into poop. It's about the same length as your height.

Your intestines are coiled up in loops and folds. That's how they fit inside you!

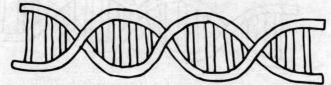

GLOSSARY

air pressure
The force of air as it pushes on things.

chemical reaction
A process where substances undergo a change to form a different substance.

electrons
Tiny specks of matter with a negative electrical charge.

evaporates
Turns from a liquid into a gas.

friction
A force that slows moving objects.

gas
A substance that is like air and has no fixed shape.

microorganism
A living creature that is too small for us to see with the naked eye, such as a bacterium.

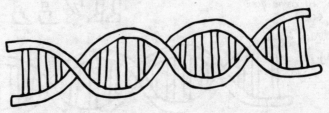

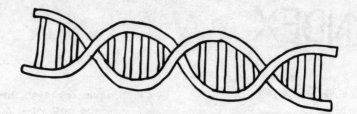

molecules
The smallest part of a substance that is still defined as that substance.

refraction
The bending of a ray of light as it passes through one substance into another, such as from air into water.

sound wave
A vibration that is produced when a sound is made, and is responsible for carrying sounds to the ear.

spore
A reproductive cell that grows into a new plant, found on ferns and fungi.

static
A form of electricity that is produced by friction.

surface tension
A force of resistance felt on the surface of a liquid.

vibrate
To move from side to side, or back and forth, very quickly.

INDEX